THE VICTORIA HISTORY OF HEREFORDSHIRE

BOSBURY

Janet Cooper with Jane Adams, Jonathan Comber, Sylvia Pinches and
David Whitehead

VICTORIA
COUNTY
HISTORY

First published 2016

A Victoria County History publication

© The University of London, 2016

ISBN 978 1 909646 25 4

Cover image: Timber-framed buildings in the main street, Bosbury, 2015. Photograph by Barry Sharples.

Back cover image: 'Picturesque Cottage' at Bosbury, from an early 20th-century Player's Cigarette card in the possession of Barry Sharples.

Typeset in Minion pro by Emily Morrell

Published with the generous support of a grant
from the Geoffrey Walter Smith Fund of
the Woolhope Naturalists' Field Club.

CONTENTS

LIST OF ILLUSTRATIONS

All photography is by Barry Sharples (unless otherwise stated) and is reproduced in this publication with his kind permission.

FOREWORD

I AM HONOURED TO BE ASKED to write a foreword to this history of Bosbury, in the County of Herefordshire, which I am proud to call home. The Victoria County History team have done a magnificent job, bringing to life at least 1,200 years of history.

Bosbury is no sleepy village. The dominant impression is a hive of activity. Although agriculture has been, and still is to the fore, national events have not passed us by. The bishops of Hereford and the Knights Templar, then the Hospitallers, have left their mark. I particularly enjoyed the picture of the Bishop's peacocks, though history does not record their fate, unlike his swans who ended up on the table. Vineyards are mentioned in the 16th century. Their time may have come again.

Ownership has been fluid even before the Reformation. Nothing has stood still. Trade was widespread and Bosbury has always been part of a broader picture. For example, the house in which I live was the result of a fortune made in North America in the 18th century and there are other similar stories.

Indeed, it could be argued that the challenge for us today is to resist the temptation to stay still, but to continue to evolve with the rest of the world.

There is much to make the reader smile – naughty vicars, pub brawls, failure to practise the long-bow (perhaps a little out of date now), illicit felling, stray animals (though there is no mention of the escaping wallabies kept by my grandfather), unlawful games during church services – the mind boggles.

At the end, there is a 'Note on Sources'. Although not necessarily the most exciting part of the book, it brings home the massive task that Janet Cooper and her team took on to uncover, decipher and bring to life our history. The acknowledgements pay tribute to the many people that tackled various parts of the task and those who have financed it. We owe them a great debt of gratitude. In particular, we should thank Bosbury's very own Barry Sharples, without whose enthusiasm the project could not have made headway.

Nathaniel Hone
HM Deputy Lieutenant of Herefordshire

ACKNOWLEDGEMENTS

THE HISTORY OF BOSBURY is the second parish history to be produced under the auspices of the Trust for the Victoria County History of Herefordshire. It continues the work on the Ledbury area which was started during the VCH-sponsored and Heritage Lottery-funded *England's Past for Everyone* project. Like the history of *Eastnor*, published in 2013, it will eventually form part of a VCH red book on Ledbury and the neighbouring Malvern Hills parishes.

The work of the Herefordshire VCH has been supported by many donors, to all of whom we are extremely grateful. Among them we should particularly like to thank Mr Roger Allsop, Dr and Mrs D.L. Booth, Dr G.T. Sennett, the D.G. Albright Charitable Trust, the William A. Cadbury Charitable Trust, the Cornus Trust, the Masefield Trust, and the John R. Murray Trust, for substantial donations during the work on Bosbury. The publication of this book has been supported by a generous gift from Barry and Sue Sharples of Bosbury, to whom we extend our sincere thanks.

The production of the Bosbury history has been a team effort. Jane Adams wrote the sections on The Poor, Education, Nonconformity, and the 19th- and 20th-century Social History, including the account of Social Life and Recreation and Inns. Jonathan Comber wrote the sections on Communications in the Introduction and Local Government in Settlement and Population, as well as contributing to parts of the accounts of early Settlement and of 19th-century Economic History. David Whitehead wrote part of the Religious Life chapter, including the accounts of the 19th-century and later church and of the church architecture; he also contributed to the sections on 18th- and 19th-century Economic and Social History. Sylvia Pinches contributed to the 19th-century Economic History and wrote the account of the 20th-century Buchanan Trust in that chapter, as well as carrying out research for all sections of the history. Janet Cooper wrote most of the remaining sections and edited the book with the assistance of Sylvia Pinches.

C.R.J. Currie visited and wrote accounts of the architecture of several of the earlier surviving domestic buildings; we are grateful to him and to the house-owners for allowing us access to their houses. Some preliminary work on vernacular buildings of the parish, carried out in 2012, was funded by a Leader+ grant.

The Herefordshire VCH volunteers, under the guidance of Sylvia Pinches, have made major contributions to the research. One group, led by Barry Sharples, photographed and transcribed all the 16th- and 17th-century wills relating to the parish; other volunteers worked on 19th-century census enumerators' books and trade directories. Barry Sharples has also created a website containing a wealth of material on Bosbury, particularly for the 18th, 19th, and 20th centuries.

Many others have been generous with their help. In particular, John Freeman has generously shared his notes on (mainly medieval) documents taken for his research on Herefordshire place-names for the English Place-Name Society. Professor Helen

Nicholson of Cardiff University and Bruce Coplestone-Crow have made available to us their work on the history of the Templar and Hospitaller manor of Upleadon and on the earlier history of the manor respectively. J.E.C. Peters has allowed us to use his notes on Nonconformist chapels. David Lovelace and John Chandler photographed documents at the National Archives.

Keith Ray organised the survey and excavation of a medieval site near the Grange. We are grateful to him and his colleagues, and to the Archaeological Research Section of the Woolhope Naturalists' Field Club for a grant towards the work.

The staff of the Herefordshire Archive Service (formerly Herefordshire Record Office) have been unfailingly helpful and are sincerely thanked. We are particularly grateful to Elizabeth Semper O'Keefe, Collections and Archives Manager, and Rhys Griffiths, the senior archivist, for allowing us access to the archives during the period in 2014–15 when they were closed in preparation for the move to new premises. We would also like to thank the staff of Hereford Cathedral Library, of the National Archives, and of the National Monuments Record for their help, and the Bosbury Parochial Church Council for giving us access to the Bosbury parish records.

Finally we would like to record our gratitude to Adam Chapman and Jessica Davies of the central VCH staff at the Institute of Historical Research, University of London, for their work on the final editing of the book and seeing it through the press.

Figure 1 *Bosbury from the air c.2000. View looking east, showing Temple Court and its orchards at the bottom, the village with Old Court and its farm buildings in the centre.*

INTRODUCTION

BOSBURY LIES IMMEDIATELY WEST of the Malvern Hills, about four miles north of the market town of Ledbury. The parish is relatively large, covering 4,827 acres or 1,953 ha.,[1] and is roughly oval in shape. For most of its history it has been divided into two manors, Bosbury and Upleadon, each of which was a separate 'division' for local government purposes until the 19th century. A third 'division', Catley, was formed from the north-eastern part of Upleadon by 1334.[2] Storridge, in Cradley, five miles to the north-east, formed part of Bosbury manor by the 1280s, and the 'hamlet' of Hazel in Tarrington parish was administered as part of Upleadon by 1308 and in 1505. From the 1470s or earlier the bishop of Hereford's lands in Bosbury, Coddington and Colwall were administered as a single manor,[3] but these arrangements were not reflected in the ecclesiastical or civil administration of the parish. In the Middle Ages Bosbury manor house was a favourite residence of the bishops of Hereford, particularly of Bishop Richard Swinfield: he had strong family connections to the area, and was at Bosbury when he died in 1317.[4] When in 1356 the cathedral chapter decided to reduce the cost of building repairs, Bosbury was one of the few episcopal manor houses they agreed to maintain.[5] From the early 16th century until the mid 19th century, when Edward Higgins created a large gentleman's residence at Bosbury House, Bosbury was without a leading resident landowner.

No major roads run through the parish, which may explain why it avoided large-scale development in the 20th century. Its perceived rural peace and its many timber-framed buildings attracted attention from antiquarians and sightseers from the late 19th century onwards. By the 1890s Bosbury featured in county guides and postcards showed the church and its detached tower, the village street, and scenic cottages. One 'old cottage in the delightfully quiet village of Bosbury' figured on a Player's cigarette card early in the 20th century.[6] Bosbury was further popularised by novelist 'Edna Lyall' (Ada Ellen Bayly), sister of Robert Burgess Bayly, vicar 1897–1906. Some pivotal scenes from her civil war drama, *In Spite of All,* were set in Bosbury churchyard and tower.[7]

1   OS Map 1:10560, 1905 edn, Herefs. sheet XXV NE; http://www.visionofbritain.org.uk (accessed 7 Oct. 2015).
2   *Lay Subsidy of 1334*, ed. R.E. Glasscock (British Academy, 1975), 128.
3   HAS, AA59/A1, p. 153; HAS, A63/III/23/1, f. 10v.; HAS, AM33/1; TNA, E 358/18.
4   *ODNB*, s.v. Richard Swinfield (accessed 3 Jun. 2016); below, Land Ownership (Bosbury House), Social Hist.
5   W.W. Capes, *Charters and Records of Hereford Cathedral* (Hereford, 1908), 226–9.
6   John Murray, *Handbook for Travellers in Worcestershire and Herefordshire* (1894), 117; H.T. Timmins, *Nooks and Corners of Herefordshire* (1892, reprinted 1974), 28–31; card in possession of Barry Sharples.
7   *ODNB* s.v. Bayly, Ada Ellen [*pseud.* Edna Lyall] (1857–1903), novelist (accessed 3 Jun. 2016); *In Spite of All* (1902).

Figure 2 *Main Street in the early 20th century. The view looking east, showing the Dog farmhouse on the left.*

Parish Boundaries

The parish boundaries, which are not known to have changed or been disputed at any date, do not follow any major natural features or roads. The southern and south-eastern boundary, with Munsley, Wellington Heath (formerly in Ledbury parish), and Coddington, follows field boundaries and then a small tributary of the Leadon to its source north-east of Coddington village. The remainder of the eastern boundary and the northern boundary, with Coddington and Mathon, follows streams; the northern boundary with Cradley and Bishop's Frome follows field boundaries to the river Leadon then a tributary stream for a short distance; the western boundary with Castle Frome, Canon Frome, and Munsley follows field boundaries. By contrast, the boundary between the manors, later divisions, of Bosbury and Upleadon (including Catley) followed the river Leadon. The boundary with Mathon was the county boundary with Worcestershire until 1897.[8]

Landscape

Bosbury contains two rather different landscapes: in the north and to a lesser extent in the east are hills divided by small streams. This hilly landscape of the northern part of the parish is reflected in the place-names Stanley Hill, Fox Hill, Beacon Hill, and Harbour Hill, the land rising to *c.*155 m. north of Fox Hill on the boundary with Castle Frome, to 146 m. at Beacon Hill near the Cradley boundary, and to 132 m. at Stanley Hill on the northern boundary with Castle Frome. Between these hills are valleys, often steep-sided with streams in their bottoms. The small river Leadon runs through the centre of the parish from north to south, entering it on the western side of Beacon Hill and flowing south to Staplow. A tributary, the Catley brook, runs south-east between Stanley Hill and Fox Hill to join the Leadon on the lower ground just north of Bosbury village. Another tributary, Dowdings brook, rises to the north-west of Beacon Hill and flows

8   OS Maps Herefs. 1:10560 028 SE, 035/NW (1887); *VCH Worcs.*, IV, 139.

south-west to join the Leadon in the village. Another stream, once called Add brook,[9] rises near Bosbury House and flows south to join the Leadon on the parish boundary. At some time before the first detailed map of the parish in 1840, and almost certainly in the Middle Ages, the courses of the river Leadon and of Dowdings brook through Bosbury village were straightened and altered to flow along the west and north sides of the bishop's manorial complex. Another channel may have been created on the eastern side of the complex, where there was still water in the early 20th century.[10]

The southern and extreme western part of the parish is flatter, more rolling countryside, sloping gently from c.75 m. at Upleadon Court near the Munsley boundary to 60–65 m. in the valleys of the Leadon and another tributary, the Stoney brook.[11] In 1850 a sale catalogue praised the 'charming and varied character' of the 'undulating landscape' around the Farm Estate between Bosbury village and Staplow.[12] The higher ground is marked by woodland, small arable fields and orchards; the lower ground by larger fields and fewer trees. The church and small village lie along the road to Cradley in the centre of the parish, on the lower ground.

The higher ground is formed of the Moors Cliffs Formation within the Lower Old Red Sandstone, a series of red-brown blocky mudstones with occasional thin calcareous sandstones, whose upper horizons are characterised by the thinly developed Chapel Point Calcrete (formerly the Bishop's Frome limestone).[13] These strata run through Bosbury from north-east to south-west. The wide bands of alluvium along the river Leadon and its tributaries, Stoney brook, Catley brook and Dowdings brook, provide plentiful meadow. The soils are typical argillic brown earths of the Bromyard series, well drained, fine, silty soils over shale and siltstone; some soils have slowly permeable subsoil and are liable to seasonal flooding; over the sandstone are some well drained, coarse loamy soils.

Communications

Apart from the short-lived Hereford and Gloucester canal, roads have been Bosbury's link with the outside world. There were a number of proposals for railways through the parish, including a broad gauge line from Worcester to Hereford in 1845, but none were built.[14] The nearest station is Ledbury.

Roads

The Ledbury to Bromyard road traverses the western side of the parish from Staplow to Stanley Hill. The section of the road in Catley was in poor condition in 1798.[15] A short distance south-west of Bosbury village the road divides, one branch continuing north-

9   HAS, AA59/A/2, f. 37.
10   The straight courses are shown on the tithe map: HAS, M5/44/9; the water to the east appears on postcards, e.g. http://www.bosburyhistoryresource.org.uk/bosbury-pictures.html (accessed 5 April 2016) but not on the tithe map.
11   OS Maps, Explorer 190, 202.
12   HAS, CN37/17.
13   British Geological Survey, Sheet no. 199. This paragraph was contributed by Dr Paul Olver.
14   Glos. Archives, Q/Rum/222 1845; Q/Rum/228 1846; Glos. Archives, D9705/5/1.
15   HAS, Q/SR/86.

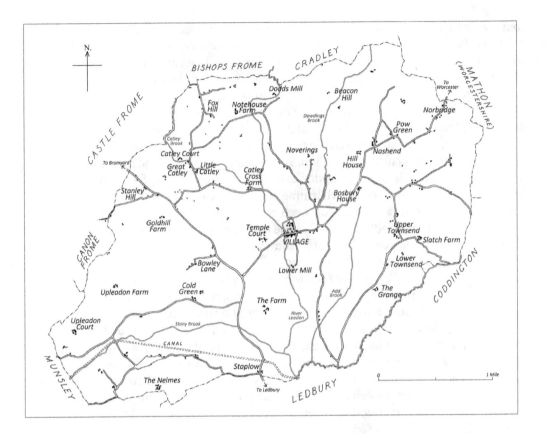

Map 1 *Bosbury parish c.1840, showing roads, rivers and streams, and the principal houses.*

west to Bromyard, the other running north-east through the village to Cradley, where it meets the main Hereford to Worcester Road. One of these, probably the Cradley road, was recorded as the king's highway in 1372.[16] The western end of the Cradley road, near Temple Court, was probably the Watery Lane whose repair was the responsibility of the residents of Upleadon in 1806; it was rebuilt before 1819.[17] A third road forked from the Cradley road north-east of the village to run south of the later Bosbury House eastwards into Coddington, and thence over the Malverns to Upton-on-Severn (Worcs.), an important inland port in the Middle Ages and later.[18] In 1578 a 'horseway' from Bosbury village to Ledbury followed the line of the minor road from the village to Wellington Heath.[19]

The Bromyard road was turnpiked in 1721 under the Ledbury Turnpike Trust Act; the Cradley road and the road to Munsley in 1838.[20] In 1838 the Coddington road was

16   *Cal. Inq. Misc.* III, no. 827.
17   HAS, Q/SR/94; Q/SR/106.
18   HAS, AA63/1, p. 311; B.S. Smith, *A History of Malvern* (Leicester, 1964) 92.
19   HAS, AA59/A/2, f. 28.
20   *Act for repairing the several roads leading to the town of Ledbury in the county of Hereford* 7 Geo. I c3;
      Annual Turnpike Acts Continuance Acts 33 & 34 Vic c73, 34 & 35 Vic c115; HAS, Q/RSL/1838; *Hereford*
      Jnl, 22 Nov. 1837, 1 from http://www.britishnewspaperarchive.co.uk (accessed 25 Aug. 2015).

diverted to run north of Bosbury House, probably to move it further away from the house which Edward Higgins was enlarging and remodelling.[21] The old road, which was still marked by farm tracks and field boundaries in 2015, would have formed a more direct route to Coddington than its replacement. A proposal in 1861 to stop another, minor, road to Coddington, from Slatch Farm, does not seem to have been acted on.[22]

There was a turnpike house at the junction of the Bromyard and Cradley roads, controlling a gate for each road. It was sold in 1871 when the roads were disturnpiked, and was demolished in 2010 after an accident which damaged the building.[23]

Bridges

There are four small bridges over the river Leadon in Bosbury: two unnamed ones in the north of the parish, England's Bridge (probably named for a 16th-century tenant)[24] near Catley Cross Farm, and another unnamed bridge on the main road at the western edge of the village. The most northerly was probably the site of the ford which gave its name to Netherford and Overford houses in 1505.[25] The now unnamed bridge in the village was probably the Bishop's bridge, frequently reported in the 1660s to be out of repair. In 1669 its repair was the responsibility of the bishop as lord of the manor.[26] In 1910 that responsibility was transferred from the bishop's successors, the Ecclesiastical Commissioners, to Herefordshire County Council, the Commissioners having first reconstructed the bridge after the fall of one of the arches. Following the rebuilding, the bridge was designated as a county bridge.[27]

Carriers

Carriers went from Bosbury to Ledbury, Worcester, Hereford and Malvern either once or twice a week at various times in the late 19th and early 20th centuries. The earliest recorded such carrier was the Bosbury man, James Fidoe, who in 1867 went to Worcester on Saturdays and to Ledbury on Tuesdays. From 1876 until at least 1902 William Parsons from Ashperton passed through Bosbury on his way to Worcester on Fridays returning the next day. In 1900 six carriers headed to Ledbury on market day (Tuesday) but by 1902 their number had declined to three. Other carriers in 1902 went to Malvern, Hereford and Worcester. No carriers are recorded after 1934.[28]

Canal

The Hereford and Gloucester canal crossed the south-western corner of the parish. The canal had opened as far as Ledbury in 1798,[29] but the section through Bosbury

21 HAS, Q/SR/126.
22 Par. Rec., vestry minutes 1 Apr. 1861; OS Map 1:25,000 sheet 190.
23 HAS, BS96/21; HAS, Q/CE/1; *Worcester News*, 19 Oct. 2010, http://www.worcesternews.co.uk/news/8459567 (accessed 16 Sept. 2015).
24 HAS, AA63/1, p. 154.
25 HAS, A63/III/23/1, f. 8v., identified from G. Gwatkin, 'Bosbury Tithe Map'.
26 HAS, AA63/1, pp. 209, 312, 369; AA63/2, pp. 23.
27 HAS, AB86/2/a 25.
28 J.B. Harrison 'Ledbury carriers': unpubl. paper based on trade directories.
29 Except where otherwise stated, this paragraph is based on D.F. Bick, *The Hereford & Gloucester Canal and the Gloucester–Ledbury Railway* (Newent, 1979).

parish was not completed until between 1841 and 1843 when the first boatload of goods reached Canon Frome Wharf. A wharf with house and weighing machine was built at Staplow.[30] The house is typical of those designed by Stephen Ballard, the canal company's engineer, of two-storeys with a curved window thought to be the look-out for the wharf clerk. Coal and timber were among the main cargoes to or from Staplow: two boats belonging to a timber-merchant of Staplow Wharf sank in the river Severn in 1867.[31] A weekly passenger boat to Ledbury market went through the parish. Staplow Wharf was still operating in 1881, when a coal merchant and a boatman lived there and a boatman was passing through on census day,[32] but the canal closed later that year when the Great Western Railway, which had gained control of it, started work to convert the Ledbury to Gloucester section into a railway.[33] A short section of the canal at Swinmore survived in 2015, as did the wharf-house, converted into a dwelling with a later 20th-century extension.

Buses

A Tuesday, market day, bus service ran from Bosbury to Ledbury from 1920 until about the 1940s.[34] In 1929 one Worcester to Hereford bus a day passed through Bosbury, with two additional services on Wednesdays and Saturdays between Worcester and Bosbury via Leigh (Worcs.) and Cradley. There were also two services between Worcester and Hereford through Bosbury on Wednesdays, Saturdays and Sundays, while on Tuesdays, there were three services between Bosbury and Ledbury, one starting or finishing in Worcester. All were operated by the Birmingham and Midland Omnibus Company Limited (Midland Red).[35] Other services, operated by Oliver Howe of Fromes Hill, included a Bromyard to Ledbury service, which probably passed through Bosbury, both before and after the Second World War.[36] In 1950 there were bus services on Tuesdays operated by Midland Red between Bosbury and Ledbury and in 1960, two services a day three days a week, with five on Tuesdays. The Cradley to Ledbury Midland Red route ceased operation in 1980.[37] In the 1990s Smith's Motors of Ledbury ran a shopping service from Ledbury to Hereford through Bosbury on Wednesdays, Hereford's market day. In 2015 there was still a Worcester to Ledbury bus service four times a day from Monday to Saturday, operated by Astons of Worcester and subsidised by Herefordshire Council. There was also a school bus from Ledbury to Bromyard via Bosbury operated by DRM Bus of Bromyard.[38]

30   *Hereford Times*, 15 Oct. 1842, 1.
31   *Hereford Jnl*, 2 Nov. 1867, 5; see also *Hereford Times*, 12 Jun. 1847, http://www.bosburyhistoryresource. org.uk (accessed 2 Dec. 2015).
32   TNA, RG 11/2581.
33   *VCH Glos.* IV, 181.
34   J.E. Dunabin, *The Hereford Bus* (1986), 36.
35   *Roadways Motor Coach and Motor Bus Timetables for England and Wales* (1929), 561–2.
36   Dunabin, *Hereford Bus*, 93.
37   Harrison, 'Ledbury Carriers'; Dunabin, *Hereford Bus*, 98.
38   Local inf.; http://www.drmbus.com/info.html (accessed 16 Sept. 2015); https://www.herefordshire.gov. uk/transport-and-highways (accessed 2 Dec. 2015), services 417, 672, 674.

Postal service and telecommunications

A gravestone in the churchyard commemorated a 'letter carrier and errand woman' who died in 1845 having served the parish for nearly 40 years.[39] A sub-post office was established in the parish in 1844; in 1851 it was in the Bell inn, and later occupied different houses in the village street. By the time it closed in 1995 it had been combined with a general store. A new post office shop opened in 1998, in the new extension to the parish hall, but closed in 2007.[40]

Telephones reached the parish sometime between 1917 and 1921. Internet access was available from April 2005.[41]

Public Services

Until the early to mid 20th century water came from the Leadon and its tributary streams, or from springs. In the 1930s water was supplied to the Grange farmhouse by a 'force pump' or by pipes from a nearby spring. The Bosbury House supply was piped from a reservoir in a neighbouring field. In 1950 Noverings House got its water from a deep well, and in 1953 Coldgreen farmhouse had an estate water supply.[42] Mains water reached the parish in 1965.[43]

Private electricity supplies were recorded from 1930, when The Grange had an 'electric light engine'. Bosbury House had a private electric plant in 1938.[44] Mains electricity reached the parish between 1945, when the church was wired for electric light, and *c*.1947.[45] Four street lamps were installed in 1965.[46] Gas mains were laid in the main street in the early 1990s, and the service was still confined to that street in 2015.[47]

Plans were drawn up in 1966 for a sewage system covering Bosbury village and land immediately to the north. Houses were connected to the system in 1969.[48]

National Events

Bosbury was briefly caught up in the rebellion of Thomas, earl of Lancaster, against Edward II and his favourites, the elder and younger Hugh Despenser. About December 1322, a rebel army led by the younger Roger Mortimer, earl of March, marched from Bromyard towards Gloucester via Ledbury. At Bosbury Mortimer held a secret meeting with the bishop of Hereford, Adam de Orleton. As a result, Orleton sent men-at-arms led

---

39   HAS, AS88/277, p. 34.
40   *Lascelles Dir. Herefs.* (1851); OS Map 1:10560 sheet xxv NE, 1905, 1926 edns; local inf. collected by Alan Starkey.
41   No telephone numbers recorded in *Kelly's Dir. Herefs.* (1917) but some in Tilley's *Ledbury Almanack* (1921); https://www.samknows.com/broadband/exchange/WNBOS (accessed 3 Jun. 2016).
42   HAS, M5/5/35, 36; HAS, AS94/209, 211 (sale catalogues).
43   WI scrapbook: http://www.bosburyhistoryresource.org.uk (accessed 19 Nov. 2015).
44   HAS, M5/5/35; HAS, AS94/211 (sale catalogues).
45   Par. Rec., PCC min. bk. 1937–65, Oct. 1945; local inf.
46   WI scrapbook, http://www.bosburyhistoryresource.org.uk (accessed 19 Nov. 2015).
47   Ex inf. Barry Sharples.
48   HAS, AD32/233–4; HAS, K42/377/22; Par. Rec., PCC min. bk. 1965–95, 26 Oct. 1969.

by nine mounted men, presumably already gathered at Bosbury, to reinforce the rebels' army.[49]

The parish also suffered during the Civil War. In the winter of 1644 Colonel Edward Massey and his Parliamentarian troops attacked Bosbury Royalists quartered at Canon Frome, capturing a captain with his cornet, some common troopers and 15 horses.[50] It was probably during disturbances surrounding this engagement that at least one house in Bosbury was ransacked and deeds stolen.[51] There is no contemporary evidence to support the later story of the vicar's saving the churchyard cross from destruction, but the 17th-century head does bear the inscription 'Honour not the + but honour God for Christ'.[52]

In the summer of 1645 the Scottish army besieging Hereford ordered nearby parishes to supply them with food. William Pullen and Richard Woodlake, the petty constables of Bosbury, used their own money and obtained credit to provide cattle, bedding and other provisions. They did so having been promised by the Scottish officers that they would be reimbursed from a general tax on the inhabitants, but no money was paid. A number of Bosbury inhabitants not only refused to contribute towards the provisioning costs but later sued Pullen and Woodlake for goods taken from them; Pullen and Woodlake in turn sought relief from the Commissioners for Indemnity.[53]

49 TNA, JUST 1/1388; *ODNB* s.v. Mortimer, Roger (V), first earl of March (1287–1330), regent, soldier, and magnate; Orleton [Hereford], Adam (c.1275–1345), diplomat, politician, and bishop (accessed 3 Jun. 2016).

50 J. Webb, *Memorials of the Civil War in Herefordshire* II, 122–3; *Bibliotheca Gloucestrensis*, ed. J. Washbourn, 132.

51 TNA, C 6/156/185.

52 Bentley, *Short Account of Bosbury* (1881), 16; Brooks and Pevsner, *Herefordshire*, 117.

53 TNA, SP 24/70.

SETTLEMENT AND POPULATION

Early Settlement

LITTLE EVIDENCE HAS SO FAR been found of prehistoric activity in the parish. Undated flints have been found north of the modern village, east of Novering's farm, and north east of Bentley's farm. Mesolithic and Neolithic flint debitage (waste flakes probably from the manufacture of blades), and a fragment of a late Neolithic or early Bronze-Age knapped flint knife have also been reported.[1] Three hut platforms and two enclosures in the south of the parish, between Staplow and Swinmore, are known only from aerial photographs and hence are undated, but they may be Roman, as pottery sherds and brooches of that date have been found in the same area.[2]

There was certainly an Anglo-Saxon settlement at Bosbury, probably by the late 8th or early 9th century, for the place name means Bosa's *burh* or enclosed place. The five recorded men called Bosa – none of them from Herefordshire – lived between the late 7th and the late 9th century,[3] indicating that the name was in use at those dates. The *burh* was probably a defensive enclosure; it may have enclosed a church and its community, including, perhaps, the bishop's house. Alternatively, as no bishop called Bosa is known, it may have been the centre of a secular estate.[4] The existence of the possibly early medieval Bosbury bell, a 'Celtic bell' now in the Horniman Museum in London, might strengthen the case for an early ecclesiastical site in the parish, but there are now doubts about its date.[5] Moreover, the circumstances in which the bell was found are obscure. It is variously said to have been bought in a sale, found in a farmhouse, or ploughed up in a field in Bosbury;[6] when it was first described, to the Society of Antiquaries in 1889, the owner said it had come from Bishampton near Pershore.[7]

1   HER 1764 and 1777; https://finds.org.uk, nos WAW 3452D3, 4AD13D, 3452D3, HESH B6FB61 (accessed 16 Mar. 2015).
2   HER 6860–1, 33793–5; https://finds.org.uk, nos WAW 2739EE, 354CBC, 26C8F2, 2646D4, E85A3E, E8257C, E7C479 (accessed 4 Nov. 2015).
3   http://www.pase.ac.uk (accessed 22 Sept. 2015). The argument put forward by Bentley, *Hist. Bosbury* (1891), 3, is based on a spurious charter, now numbered S189: http://www.esawyer.org.uk (accessed 22 Sept. 2015).
4   See S. Draper, 'The significance of OE Burh in Anglo-Saxon England', *Anglo-Saxon Studies in Archaeology and History* 15 (2008), 231–6; S. Keynes, 'Diocese and Cathedral before 1056', *Hereford Cathedral*, ed. G. Aylmer and J. Tiller (London, 2000), 3–21.
5   Email from Keeper of Musical Instruments, Horniman Museum, to Dr Sylvia Pinches, Jul. 2009.
6   HER 1756; Bentley, *Hist. Bosbury* (1891), 76; E.M. Leather, *Folklore of Herefs.* (1912), 169.
7   *Proceedings of the Soc. of Antiquaries of London*, 12 (1889), 416.

Population from 1086

By 1086 the later parish contained two separate estates, Bosbury and Upleadon, each
with its own manorial centre, presumably on the sites of the later manor houses
which stood on either side of the river Leadon in the centre of the parish. Other small
settlements were scattered round the parish. Domesday book recorded 34 tenants,
presumably heads of households, and two slaves on the bishop of Hereford's Bosbury
manor, and 45 tenants and six slaves on the Upleadon estate, which took its name from
the river.[8] If households averaged 4–5 persons, the numbers would suggest populations of
at least 150 in Bosbury and at least 200 in Upleadon.

Bosbury, with its associated episcopal manors of Colwall and Coddington, was later
said to have suffered severely from the Black Death, 158 tenants having died on the three
manors; certainly at least two vicars died.[9] In 1377 92 people aged 14 or over paid poll tax
in Bosbury and the same number in Upleadon and Catley,[10] suggesting a total population
in each township of c.140, a reduction in the probable Domesday populations. In
1505 there were 44 messuages on the Hospitallers' Upleadon manor, but also 14 tofts,
at least one of which had formerly been a messuage.[11] By 1547 there were 220 (adult)
communicants in the parish.[12] A rental of the bishop's manor made in 1578 recorded only
12 'built' customary or copyhold houses, compared to 18 'unbuilt' or decayed houses, and
eight 'built' freehold houses with a further six 'unbuilt'.[13] The figures suggest continued
decline, at least on that manor, but probably do not include houses on the bishop's
demesne.

The parish registers suggest a growing population from the later 16th century,[14]
baptisms exceeding burials even in 1578 and 1579, and 1587 and 1588 perhaps epidemic
years, when there were 13 and 14 burials respectively, double the usual number. Deaths
were high again, up to 25 per year, in 1609, between 1612 and 1616, and in 1631.
The population had recovered by 1676 when a total of 302 adults was reported in the
parish, suggesting a total population of c.450.[15] The years 1704–13, 1727–9 and 1766–7,
were periods of high mortality which no doubt temporarily reduced the population.
Otherwise the 18th century seems to have been a time of growth. On Bosbury manor,
a cottage had been built in a field by 1700; a 'lately erected' cottage, probably in or near
the village, was recorded in 1707, and a new house at Strode's moor in 1734. In 1765
there was a general complaint about encroachments on the lord's waste on the manors
of Bosbury, Colwall and Coddington, and by 1770 three cottages had been built on the
waste at Birchwood near the northern edge of the parish.[16]

8   *Domesday*, 502, 512; B. Coplestone-Crow, *Herefordshire Place-names* (Logaston, 2009), 49.
9   M.G. Watkins, *Collections towards the History and Antiquities of the County of Hereford, in Continuation of Duncumb's History*, V, part 2 (1902), 28; below Religious Hist. The earliest record of this tradition is in the parish registers for the later 16th century.
10 *The Poll Taxes of 1377, 1379 and 1381*, ed. C.C. Fenwick (British Academy, 1998), vol 1, 358.
11 HAS, A63/III/23/1, ff. 7v.–10v.
12 HCA, 6450/2, p. 27 (transcript of TNA, E 301/24).
13 HAS, AA59/A2, ff. 1–53v.
14 Except where otherwise stated the following paragraph is based on Par. Rec., registers of baptisms and burials.
15 *The Compton Census of 1676*, ed. A. Whiteman (British Academy, 1986), 260.
16 HAS, AA63/5, p. 24; AA63/6, p. 247; AA63/11, p. 37; AA63/15, p. 216; AA63/15, p. 86.

In 1801 the population of the parish was 776. It grew to a peak of 1137 in 1841, and was little changed at 1133 in 1851. Thereafter it declined steadily to 852 in 1911; after a slight rise to 871 in 1921, it declined again to a low point of 637 in 1971. In 1981 it was 758, but had fallen to 727 in 1991, the last year for which separate figures are available. In 2011 the population of Bosbury, with Coddington, was 813.[17]

Medieval and Later Settlement

There was probably some concentration of medieval settlement beside the Leadon, near the church and the Bosbury and Upleadon manor houses, but other houses or groups of houses were scattered over the parish. The two largest may have been at Catley (cats' wood), in the north of the parish, which was first recorded in 1243, having earlier been part of Upleadon,[18] and at Staplow. Staplow, recorded as a surname in the 15th century and as an area of Upleadon in 1505, lies on the parish southern boundary, and its place-name, meaning 'post mound' or 'post tumulus,'[19] suggests an early boundary mark. A canal wharf was built there in the early 1840s.[20]

A rental of the bishop's manor made c.1288 records four men surnamed de la Broke, who may have lived near the later Brookend, recorded from 1669 near Dowdings Brook, just north of Bosbury village.[21] Thomas and Ralph de la Esse [Ash] may have been at the later Nash End, north-east of the village, and Adam, William and Roger de Birchill near Birchwood in the north-east corner of the parish. The three people surnamed de la Strode occupied land at or near Strowde hill, possibly the later Tupsley hill which lay north of the village and south-west of Beacon Hill.[22]

Two field names recorded in a survey of the bishop's manor in 1578 are suggestive of early settlement: Oldebury a parcel of demesne land immediately south of Bosbury village, and Turtellsbury Acre, in South field adjoining 'Ledbury horseway', possibly south of the modern farm The Grange.[23] Excavations in a field north-west of The Grange, formerly part of the demesne arable, have revealed an undocumented house or farmstead. The use of stone in at least part of the structure suggests that it was of relatively high status; it was occupied from the mid 12th to the mid 14th century. There may have been another house, within a moat, further south and west in the same field.[24]

By 1578 there were two or more houses, or house sites, at Nashend, at Townsend (extending across the parish boundary into Coddington), at Noverend (modern

17   *Census* 1801–1991; http://neighbourhood.statistics.gov.uk/dissemination/LeadTableView.
      do?a=7&b=11120940&c=bosbury&d=16&g=6385925&i=1001x1003x1006&k=population&m=0&r=1&
      s=1468266880766&enc=1&domainId=58&dsFamilyId=2473&nsjs=true&nsck=false&nssvg=false&
      nswid=1508 (accessed 12 July 2016).
18   *Book of Fees*, II, 808; B. Coplestone-Crow, *Herefordshire Place-names*, 49; below Land Ownership.
19   Inf. from John Freeman, citing St Katherine's deed in cathedral library; HAS, A63/III/23/1, ff. 7v., 8; M.
      Gelling and A. Cole, *The Landscape of Place-names* (Stamford, 2000), 178–80, 188.
20   Above, Introduction (Communications).
21   HAS, AA59/A1, pp. 153–9; AA59/A2, f. 44v.; HAS, AA63/2, p. 50.
22   HAS, AA59/A2, ff. 29v., 46v. The place-name Stroud Patch appears on tithe map on the northern parish
      boundary: Gwatkin, 'Bosbury Tithe Map'.
23   HAS, AA59/A2, ff. 28, 54v.
24   Unpubl. interim report by Dr Keith Ray.

Noverings), at Pow Green, at Birchend, and at Brookend. The largest settlements, containing four or five houses, were at Nashend and at Townsend.[25]

What evidence there is suggests that the early settlement pattern in Upleadon was similar to that in Bosbury, though without any groups of houses. In a rental of 1505 Much and Little Allways (near the modern The Farm), two houses called Godmans or Goodmans land, and a house and a cottage at Hokerhill are the only clear instances of two houses near each other, but few of the houses in the rental can be identified.[26] A freehold house called Nelmes, recorded in 1505 and 1548, and conveyed to a new owner in 1598, was presumably on the site of the modern The Nelmes, on the southern boundary with Munsley. A house at Staplow recorded in 1551 was held with a Hill House, perhaps in the later Hill Croft near Cold Green, and a house in Catley.[27] The house called Hockerhill, recorded in 1505 but ruinous and in need of repair in 1587, seems to have disappeared without trace. Two houses seem to have been in 'ends', perhaps comparable to Nashend and Townsend in Bosbury: houses in Beriend, possibly near the manorial centre, in 1505 and 1587 and one at Woodyend in 1613.[28] The cottage called Flea Hill, which stood in a field of the same name in 1649, was probably recently built, as perhaps was the house in a 7-a. close near the boundary with Munsley sold in 1707.[29]

The modern village of Bosbury lies mainly along the south side of the street opposite the parish church. The closely built houses, mainly of the 16th–18th centuries, with their long narrow gardens give the appearance of a planned village, or even of a small market town although there was never a market.[30] The village was extended in the 20th century, first by 10 council houses, known as Morton Cottages, which were completed in 1947, and then by a total of 58 houses, some council houses and some private bungalows, built at Forge Bank, the site of the former forge. An application in 2014 to build a further 46 houses on land behind the school, south of the village, was refused.[31] The most prominent 20th-century addition to the village was the single-storey, brick, parish hall built in 1968 west of the church on the site of the former vicarage house. It was extended in 1998.[32]

Elsewhere in the parish, scattered farmhouses and clusters of smaller houses remain, some probably on sites occupied since the Middle Ages. Already in 1754 the Cradley road at Norbridge was lined with houses, and by the mid 19th century, there were small groups of houses on the same road at Pow Green, and along the Bromyard road at Stanley Hill and at Bowley Lane; from 1861 other houses were built around the

25   HAS, AA63/6, p. 136. The 'town' from which the end took its name may have been Coddington rather than Bosbury.

26   HAS, A63/III/23/1, ff. 7v.–10v.

27   TNA, LR 3/21/3; TNA, SC 2/176/102; HAS, A63/III/23/1, f. 9v.; HAS, A81/II/86; Gwatkin, 'Bosbury Tithe Map'.

28   TNA, LR 3/21/3; HAS, A63/III/23/1, f. 7v.; HAS, A81/II/89.

29   HAS, A81/II/96, 100.

30   HAS, M5/44/9 (tithe map); S. Letters (ed.), *Gazetteer of Markets and Fairs in England and Wales to 1516*, http://www.history.ac.uk/cmh/gaz/gazweb2.html (accessed 30 Sept. 2015).

31   https://www.herefordshire.gov.uk/planning-and-building-control (accessed 26 Nov. 2015).

32   http://www.bosburyparishhall.org (accessed 17 Nov. 2015); below, Social History (parish hall), Religious History (vicarage house).

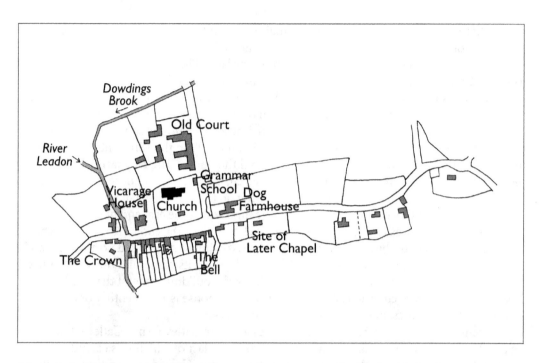

Map 2 Bosbury village c.1840, showing the row of houses opposite the church with their long, narrow gardens.

newly inclosed Swinmore Common.[33] Before 1944 the council built two blocks of semi-detached houses, the first council houses in the parish, at Cold Green.[34]

The Built Environment

Like its neighbouring parishes, Bosbury contains many timber-framed houses originally built between the 16th and the 18th centuries. Most houses of this period were probably originally of four rooms, two on the ground floor and two above: 42 out of the 62 householders assessed for hearth tax in 1665 were assessed on only one or two hearths.[35] Such houses were presumably like that occupied in 1669 by a widow who had a hall and parlour with chambers over them and a kitchen, or the house described in an inventory of 1681 which had a parlour, hall and buttery with chambers over the hall and buttery.[36] Other houses were even smaller; two poor men who died in 1676 each had a hall and parlour or kitchen with only a single chamber above.[37] On the other hand, the house

33   TNA, HO 107/1975; TNA, RG 9/1809; RG 10/2681; I. Taylor, *Map of Herefs.*, http://www. bosburyhistoryresource.org.uk (accessed 2 Dec. 2015); OS Map 1:10560, 035 NE, SE (1886 edn).
34   Par. Rec., burial register, 4 Aug. 1944.
35   HAS Libr., TS transcript of 1665 hearth tax by J. Harnden, 68, 83.
36   HAS, 23/1/20, will of Anne Burgess, 1669; 70/2/30, will of George Warner 1681.
37   HAS, 48/2/9, will of James Makeham 1676; 52/2/50, will of John Hawfield 1676.

of another widow, Joan Powell, in 1663 contained a painted chamber, and the yeoman
Arthur Booth, in 1674 had a chamber called paradise.[38]

Most of the houses date from the 16th century or later. They include Lower Townend
(below), Upper Townend of *c*.1600, and Notehouse Farm in Catley, an L-shaped house part
of which may date to the late 16th century.[39] Upleadon Farm, of the late 16th or early 17th
century, was originally built on a modified form of the medieval hall house plan, with two
rooms on each floor. The passage between them, however, led to the spiral stairs, not to a
back door. The mortices for the high seat survive in the hall. In the 18th century another
room, with an upper cruck roof, was added beyond the stairs.[40] The Dog farmhouse on the
north side of Bosbury's main street east of the church, is another hall house, comprising
hall and service area of three bays with a cross-wing on the east. The hall was originally
open to the roof, and part of the canopy over the high seat at the east end of the hall
survives. The house was extensively altered in the late 16th or the early 17th century when
the hall was floored. In the late 17th century the cross-wing was extended northwards, and
in the 18th century the house was adapted for hop drying.[41] Its name, and the fact that the
tithe map of 1840 shows a moat round three sides of the building, suggest that the Moats,
near Townend, may occupy an early site. The surviving house is 17th-century or earlier,
single-storey with attics; in the 1930s it was two cottages.[42]

Among the many other 17th-century houses are four Catley farms: Catley Court
of *c*.1600, Great and Little Catley, and Catley Cross, the last of which was extended in
the late 17th or the early 18th century. Coldgreen Farm in Upleadon, and Lower House
Farm, north of Bosbury village are also 17th-century. Palace Farm, near the Coddington
boundary, retains much of its original appearance: it comprises a two-bay hall with cross-
wing, the hall jettied to the front. Goldhill Farmhouse at Stanley Hill on the Bromyard
road, was originally an L-shaped, 17th-century house, but was altered in the 18th century
and refaced in the 19th.

Two substantial 18th-century houses, Nashend (below) and Bosbury House (below)
were built or remodelled by members of the Stedman family who acquired a large estate
in the north-east of the parish in the 1780s. Another two houses were rebuilt in the
early 19th century: The Farm, off the Ledbury road between Bosbury and Staplow,[43] and
Upleadon Court, in the extreme south-west of the parish.[44]

The Grange was largely rebuilt in 1889 by the London architect G.M. Silley for Samuel
Wilcox.[45] Noverings House was built, on a different site from the earlier farmhouse,
c.1907 for Mrs Marian Buck. She continued to develop the Noverings estate in the 1920s

38   HAS, 20/1/35, will of Joan Powell, 1663; 41/3/23, will of Arthur Booth 1674.
39   NHL, nos 1156869, Notehouse and adjoining granary; 1098922, The Townend; 1156813, Lower
      Townend (accessed 5 Oct. 2015). Lack of resources prevented staff from examining more than a few
      houses in detail.
40   J.W. Tonkin, 'An introduction to the houses of Herefordshire', *TWNFC*, 39 (1968), 189, 191, 193; idem,
      'Buildings', *TWNFC*, 40 (1971), 286.
41   J.W. Tonkin, 'Buildings', *TWNFC*, 49 (1997), 134; above Figure 2.
42   NHL no. 1098902, The Moats (accessed 3 Jun. 2016).
43   Brooks and Pevsner, *Herefordshire*, 118. The house was 'of modern construction' in 1850: HAS,
      CN37/17, sale cat.
44   The house is not on an estate map of 1791 (HAS, AS80/15), but is shown on the OS map 1:3 360, 1st edn
      (1831): http://www.bosburyhistoryresource.org.uk (accessed 3 Dec. 2015).
45   Brooks and Pevsner, *Herefordshire*, 118; Par. Rec., sale cat. (1937).

and 1930s, building a new cottage at Little Noverings and two villas at Littlecroft and Maycroft, all in a rather idiosyncratic style.[46] Little new building occurred in Bosbury village during the 19th century. The most significant was the erection, probably *c.*1870, of commercial premises on the south of the main street, near the bridge. This brick building, with coloured brick details, housed the New Inn and the post office. The property was sold in 1922 and the inn converted into a private house; in 2015 it was two separate dwellings.[47]

After the First World War the Buchanan Trust built new cottages and farmsteads for ex-servicemen at Orchard Farm, Aurals Farm, Aurals cottage, Birchwood Farm, North farm and Beacon Hill farm. Some of the farm buildings were made of shuttered concrete.[48]

Domestic Architecture

Old Court

The house and farm buildings stand on the site of the bishop's manor house.

Figure 3 *Old Court gatehouse 2015, showing the 13th-century archway with the blocked pedestrian gateway adjoining.*

46   HAS, M5/5/35, 36 (sale cats.); HAS, AG9/46, land valuation 1910.
47   HAS, CJ22/3 plan of New Inn and Post Office, 1887; HAS, AS94/213 sale notice; TNA, RG 14/15602; ex inf. Peter Young, occupier in 2015.
48   TNA, WORK 6/187/11; TNA, MAF 48/311; MAF 174/106. For the Trust see below, Economic Hist.

The oldest part is the gatehouse, on the road which runs from Bosbury to Catley, along the eastern side of the churchyard.[49] The earliest phase of the structure appears to be late 13th-century and to include the stone exterior eastern arch of the gatehouse, the now blocked pedestrian gate adjoining it on the south, and the side walls of the gatehouse proper. A second, timber archway closed the gatehouse at the west end; its northern post rests on the stone plinth, but the southern post rests on a pad stone set on the ground. The tops of the posts are unjowelled, and the wall plates of the west wall, which was evidently timber-framed, were morticed into them. The two arched gateways rose through two full storeys. A contemporary chimney, whose remains survive immediately south of the pedestrian gate, served a first-floor fireplace whose hood corbels remain, indicating that the range was two-storeyed. Immediately to the south on the ground floor are the jambs and part of the hood of another fireplace, probably served by a flue in the wall or projecting from it, which heated the ground-floor room. The front (east) wall of this range was of stone. The north wall of the gatehouse has a high stone plinth supporting timber framing; the south wall is of stone to first-floor level. Many rafters of a collar-rafter roof, which may have been the original roof of the range, have been reused in the surviving 18th-century roof. In the 18th century and later the buildings were remodelled for hop processing and considerably extended.

The bishop transacted business in his hall in 1279, and in his chamber in 1346. In 1293 or 1294 the chamber at the upper end of the hall and the lord's chamber were repaired, as were a barn, a bake-house, and a fence towards the cellar.[50] In 1503 Bishop Mayew leased to Thomas Morton, archdeacon of Hereford, and Rowland Morton the houses under one roof lying between the churchyard and the hall, and all the houses and the dovecote on the north side of a wall from the chapel to the stable. The bishop reserved to his own use, or rather that of his servants, two chambers above the granaries, the slaughterhouse on the north side of the stable, the western half of the great barn which was separated from the rest of the barn by a timber partition, half the hay barn 'towards the north' and a granary. In 1563 Bishop Scory gave the then lessee, Richard Harford, licence to demolish all but the farm buildings, the houses being ruinous and in a moist, 'unwholesome' position.[51]

Harford did not demolish all the houses, however, as the earliest part of the surviving farmhouse, the south range, dates from the 15th century. It is rather too far from the gatehouse to have been part of the bishop's main residence, and may have been the 'farmer's house' recorded in 1578.[52] If so, it was probably that later occupied by the gentleman John Danett (d. 1679) which contained a hall, great parlour, little parlour, dining room, and kitchen, with parlour chamber, closet, master chamber, red chamber, kitchen chamber, chamber adjoining the servants' chamber, chamber over the servant maids' chamber, the menservants' chamber and a cockloft, as well as Danett's study and 'lodging'.[53] At the east end of the surviving south range is a parlour of three bays of elaborately moulded joists supported by moulded ceiling beams. The western bay has

49 This and the following paragraphs are by Dr C.R.J. Currie, based on his examination of the buildings in Aug. 2015.
50 *Reg. Cantilupe*, 197; *Reg. Trillek*, 78; HCA R366.
51 *Reg. Mayew*, 8; HAS, AA59/A2, ff. 60v.–61.
52 HAS, AA59/A2, f. 27; see also NMR, RCHME index cards, Bosbury Old Court.
53 HAS, 63/1/5, will of John Danett, 1679.

been truncated by the insertion of the chimney and later partitioning. The western room beyond the chimney is now featureless and has served as a kitchen. Upstairs it had two two-bay open rooms on the first floor with a single bay between. The open rooms have arched braced open trusses, and the closed partition trusses had tie beams, collar, and struts; the tie beam of at least one partition truss has been replaced.[54] The south wall was refaced and refenestrated in the 19th century. The house was extended to the north, possibly in the 16th century, but only fragmentary walling survives, as that wing was almost completely rebuilt in brick c.1800.

Temple Court

The house stands in a dry moat, still complete in 1920, but much modified by modern gardening. The earliest part of the building is the western two-thirds of the north wing, with stone walls some 82–86 cm. (2ft. 8 ins. to 2 ft. 10 ins.) thick, which may have formed the lower part of a chamber block of the 13th-century manor house. The northern wall includes two deeply-splayed doorways, of which one was probably at first a window, since the lintel has two sets of holes for mullions including apparent central shafts. The south wall is shorter than the north; its east end may have been timber-framed: the block was extended to the east in the Middle Ages with a two-storeyed, timber-framed bay in large panelled framing, apparently jettied at the east front. Perhaps in the 17th century, following decay of the timber, the framing was replaced in stone and further extended to the east; the first-floor bressumer on the north side remains encased in the wall. The medieval hall range probably abutted the stone on the south, where a late 16th- or 17th-century kitchen chimney survives. In the mid 18th century a five-bayed south-facing east–west brick range of two storeys and attics, with two main rooms on either side of a staircase hall and end chimney stacks, was added at the south end of the kitchen range, and in the late 19th century the latter was completely replaced with a brick block joining the south and north ranges, incorporating the kitchen stack, and perhaps re-using some ceiling timbers. Perhaps at the same time the roofs of the front range were modified to provide deep projecting eaves.[55]

The Bell

The 15th-century house contained an open hall of two equal bays parallel to the village street; its arched-braced collar-beam central truss survives in what is now a first-floor room. At the south end is a bay projecting into the street with a gable over; the gable carries barge boards with quatrefoil cusped ornament. The hall was ceiled c.1600. Extensions, originally outbuildings, at the west end appear to date from the 18th century. At the north end of the range is a separate structure, a timber-framed house of the 17th or 18th century.

Lower Townend

The house stands in an isolated site at the end of a lane. The ground falls away sharply to the west of the house. The first phase dates from the 15th century and consists of an open

54   J.W. Tonkin, 'The palaces of the bishop of Hereford', *TWNFC*, 42 (1976), 56–7; investigator's photographs (2015).
55   See NMR, RCHME record card.

Figure 4 *Lower Townend from the north-east, 2015, showing the small projection at the east end of the hall.*

hall with two equal bays and an arched-braced collar-beam open truss with moulded pilasters rising to moulded capitals from above which the arched braces spring. Above the collar are V-struts framing cusped and foiled openings. At the east end is a small projection apparently contemporary with the hall and possibly part of a canopy over the dais bench. At the west end there was an additional bay or cross wing incorporating a cross entry flanked by a frame with chamfered rail, under which was the entry to the hall. About 1600 the hall was ceiled and a chimney, surmounted by four diagonal flues with brick fillets, inserted at the west end. The chimney has a wide ground-floor fire place with stone jambs whose mouldings are returned round a timber head. The ceiling beams have wide chamfers and extend into the eastern projection. A straight stair rose north of the chimney to a new door to the west bay or wing. In the chamber above the hall a dormer window near the south-east corner may be also of *c.*1600, though later modernized; it has partially combed plasterwork with shallow moulded ornaments in the dormer gable inside, and similar plasterwork is above the first-floor fireplace, which has a plain chamfered surround and timber lintel. Later alterations included the reframing of the south wall in panels of four heights and the demolition of the west bay or wing. In the late 20th century extensions were built on the site of the west bay or wing and at the east end.

Figure 5 *The panelled room at the Crown c.1930, showing the mid 16th-century ceiling beams with their bosses and the slightly later panelling.*

The Crown

The surviving house formed the south wing of the house built by John and Richard Harford in the mid 16th century;[56] the remainder of the house was demolished and rebuilt in the 18th century. John Harford (d. 1559) probably built the stone side walls; the front and south walls were probably timber-framed: small fragments of the framing remain inside the house. He was probably also responsible for the ceiling beams, in double cross pattern, in the ground floor room. At intersections of the beams were bosses; the three surviving ones bear the arms of William Paulet first marquis of Winchester, John Skippe, bishop of Hereford 1539–52 and the quartered coat of Scrope (for John's wife Anne, daughter of Sir John Scrope). John's son Richard (d. 1578), probably *c.*1571, cased the front and rear walls with three-foot thick stone walls and built a collar-rafter roof, each couple having two collars with soulaces to the lower collar. The roof was probably intended to support an ornate plaster ceiling in the upper chamber. The lower chamber was lined with plank and muntin panelling with an enriched cornice and an ornate overmantle inscribed 'RH & MH 1571' for Richard and Martha Harford, and containing the arms of Wrottesley (for Anne Harford's mother), Scrope and Fox (for Martha Harford, the daughter of Charles Fox).[57] In 1576 the house comprised the 'parlour within the hall', the little parlour, and the new parlour, with the high chamber,

56   HAS, AA59/A/2, f. 29.
57   RCHM, *Herefordshire*, ii. 19; Bentley, *Hist. Bosbury* (1891), 40.

Figure 6 *Hill House Farm from the south-west, 2015, showing the successive extensions of the original hall, including the 17th-century staircase block.*

new chamber, Mr Arden's chamber, hall chamber, maids' chamber, malt chamber, kitchen chamber, next chamber, as well as the kitchen and brew house.[58]

Hill House

The house was probably newly built on its present site some time between 1590 and 1610: the house described in a survey of 1578 appears to have been a bit further north.[59] The first phase included a short hall range, timber-framed, with the first floor slightly jettied over an ovolo-moulded bressumer, on the north side, and an ornate, two-storeyed, east cross wing, with timber framing of close studding and lozenge panels between stone lower blocks. The posts also have ovolo mouldings. The wing has a contemporary, lateral chimney to the east. The main range appears to have had a smoke bay or a smoke hood before the present north chimney and fireplace with moulded surround was added, probably in the early 17th century. The house was enlarged westwards by successive additions, in timber framing on stone ground walls, in the 17th and 18th centuries, and *c.*1700 a three-storeyed south staircase block was added at the corner of the hall range with the wing. The dog-leg staircase has original moulded rail and balusters with close strings. It may have been the work of one of the two Francis Romneys, gentlemen who occupied the house from 1671 to 1728.[60] The western extension included a granary, and a barn which was demolished in the 20th century.

58   TNA, PROB 11/58, will of Richard Harford, 1576.
59   HAS, AA59/A2, f. 42.
60   HAS, AA63/2, p.135; AA63/7, p. 65; AA63/10, p. 143.

Nashend House

A stone and timber rear range survives from an earlier, probably 18th-century, house.[61] Any structures at the south end of that house were replaced by a three-bay brick house of two-storeys and cellars built *c*.1800, presumably by John Stedman who acquired the house in 1787.[62] It has a symmetrical façade with central doorway and end chimneys; there is a 'Gothick' traceried fan-light over the door and in the head of the central first-floor window.

Bosbury House

The south-western end of the present house may have been preceded by a much earlier house whose timbers were extensively re-used in a later roof; the remains include many smoke-blackened timbers, some apparently from an open hall with a crown-post roof of the 14th century, and also timbers from unheated structures, perhaps one or more cross wings with upper chambers, including an elaborately moulded cornice of *c*.1500, and one principal rafter of an arch-braced collar-beam truss of that date or earlier. Further to the north-east, a large kitchen chimney of the 16th or 17th century was enclosed in the north block in the 18th century; it had perhaps been part of a wing whose south-eastern projection survived in the 1880s.

The earliest clearly identifiable part of the house, however, is the early 18th-century brick north-east range, of one storey and attics, with platbands below the north gable; it probably contained servants' quarters or service rooms. In the mid 18th century a four-bay square brick range was added or rebuilt to its north-west, incorporating the kitchen.

About 1800 John Stedman, or his brother and successor Philip, extended that range to the south-west with another square block on its north-west and south-west fronts, of two storeys and cellars and five bays, and a slightly recessed bay to the north, joining it to the north-west front of the north block. It had a central staircase hall lit on the rear, south-east side by a tall window with semicircular head and Gothick-traceried glazing bars. That new block re-used material from the medieval house, which it probably replaced, in its roof. It was further extended by one bay to the south-west in the 19th century, perhaps by Edward Higgins, to create a more symmetrical north-west façade; it was perhaps then that the north block was reroofed and partly refaced, and a balustraded parapet was added round the south-west block.

A small rear courtyard between the south-west block and the kitchen wing survived in the 1880s, but between 1912 and 1913 it was filled in with a tall three-storeyed bathroom tower with concrete upper floors to support large lead water tanks, and the kitchen wing was truncated west of the north-east range and reroofed from north-west to south-east. At the same period the main staircase was rebuilt, an atrium created east of it, and much new fielded panelling added in the south-west block. The architect was O.D. Black of Liverpool.[63] Later 20th-century alterations include some refenestration, and a new doorway on the north-west front of the north block.

---

61   NHL no. 1098919, Nash End farmhouse (accessed 5 Oct. 2015); it was not possible to examine this wing.

62   HAS, AA63/15, p. 33.

63   Brooks and Pevsner, *Herefordshire*, 118.

The outhouses north-east of the house include a 17th-century stone building at the north-east end, extended in brick south-westwards in the 18th, 19th and 20th centuries.

Landownership

Bosbury Manor

The bishops of Hereford had an estate at Bosbury by 1056 when Bishop Athelstan died there. They retained the manor until it was taken over by the Ecclesiastical Commissioners in 1848, except in 1322 and between 1324 and 1327 when Edward II seized all the episcopal estates after Bishop Orleton's support of the rebellion against Edward II.[64] Some lands in Bosbury were among those assigned to the see of Hereford in 1880.[65]

The bishops retained Bosbury in their own hands until the early 16th century. Thereafter they granted long leases of the manor and manor house to a series of, mainly non-resident, lessees. In 1503 Bishop Mayew leased part of the manor house and lands to Thomas Morton (d. 1511), then archdeacon of Hereford, and Rowland, later Sir Rowland, Morton. Rowland, who later acquired The Grange (below) and Massington manor in Ledbury, was a benefactor of the parish.[66] In 1528 Bishop Bothe leased the whole manor to John Johnson. The chapter confirmed a further lease to Johnson in 1534, and leases to John Harford in 1542 (the reversion of Johnson's lease), 1551 and 1555, and to Richard Harford in 1565.[67] Further leases were granted to Elizabeth Harford in 1606, and to another Elizabeth Harford, widow of Bridstock Harford, in 1674 and 1686. In 1692 the second Elizabeth Harford settled her interest in the estate on the daughters of her first marriage, to John Danett: Elizabeth, wife of Thomas Penoyre, and Anne, wife of William Bodenham. In 1709 William Bodenham and Anne, who had presumably acquired Elizabeth's share, conveyed the lease to Thomas Brydges. The bishop leased the premises to Brydges, then of Ledbury, in 1747. Thomas, by his will of 1750, devised it to his nephew William Brydges. William, by will proved in 1762, devised the estate, then called Old Court, to his wife Mary for her life with remainder to their children. The bishop granted a new lease to Mary Brydges and her daughters Elizabeth and Mary in 1797. In the same year Mary, Elizabeth and Mary Brydges sold their interest in Old Court to Philip Stedman of The Razees (later Bosbury House), and the bishop granted a new lease to Stedman. In 1817 the bishop again leased the estate to Philip Stedman, and in 1823 he leased Old Court to the trustees under Philip Stedman's will.[68] Stedman's

64   D. Whitelock (ed.), *The Anglo-Saxon Chronicle: a Revised Translation* (Westport, CT, 1961), 132 n.; *Domesday*, 502; Bentley, *Hist. Bosbury* (1891), 24; *ODNB* s.v. Orleton [Hereford], Adam (*c.*1275–1345), diplomat, politician, and bishop (accessed 3 Jun. 2016); *Cal. Pat.* 1321–24, 452; *Cal. Fine*, 1319–27, 307.
65   *London Gaz.*, 8 Aug. 1880, 4458–9.
66   *Reg. Mayew*, 8; *Fasti Ecclesiae Angicanae 1300–1541*, II, *Hereford Diocese*, http://www.british-history.ac.uk (accessed 28 Dec. 2015); *ODNB*, s.v. Morton, Sir William (*bap.* 1605, *d.* 1672), judge and politician (accessed 3 Jun. 2016); below, Social History.
67   *Reg. Bothe*, 206; HCA, P.G.S. Baylis, 'Transcript of Chapter Act Bk' I, nos 482, 658; II, nos 818, 929, 1184.
68   HAS, HD1/4, 5, 6, 7, *passim*.

trustees probably sold their interest in Old Court, for in 1823 the estate was said to belong to John Barber, who still held it in 1839.[69]

The Rectory Estate

A priest held a hide, presumably rectorial glebe, of the bishop's manor in 1086. In the 1280s eleven free and three unfree tenants held small amounts of land of the rectory or parsonage. After the appropriation of the rectory c.1276, the land was administered with the rest of the bishop's estate.[70]

Bosbury House, earlier Raceys

A survey made c.1280 records three tenants by knight service on the bishop's Bosbury manor, each holding a yardland, one of whom was Roger Racy. Roger or one of his successors received a legacy from his (or her) cousin Bishop Richard Swinfield (d. 1317), apparently as late as 1346.[71] In 1427 or 1428 Thomas Delabere, a member of a Herefordshire knightly family, acquired the estate. About 1500 it was held by Richard Delabere, who was succeeded by his son Thomas (d. 1518) and then by Thomas's daughter Elizabeth, wife of Michael Lister. Her infant son Richard Lister held the estate in 1533. By 1578 John Hope owned the estate; he or another man of the same name, then living in Ledbury, leased or mortgaged Raceys c.1606.[72] About 1786 the estate, then called The Razees, was acquired by John Stedman (d. 1809) who later acquired another house and land at Nashend.[73] He was succeeded in both estates by his brother Philip (d. 1820), who, by will proved in 1822, devised his lands to trustees to sell.[74] The trustees sold the estate c.1828 to the Revd Edward Higgins.[75] Higgins died in 1884, and was succeeded by Willoughby Baskerville Mynors, son of his daughter Ellen Gray and her husband Robert Baskerville Mynors.[76] Willoughby Baskerville Mynors's library and other possessions at Bosbury House were sold in 1911,[77] and the estate was acquired by Robert Buchanan, who in 1918 and 1919 gave c.788 a. of the land at Nashend to found the Bosbury Farm Settlement for former soldiers.[78] Bosbury House was sold in 1938 to Thomas Nathaniel Hone, whose family still owned it in 2015.[79]

---

69 HAS, Q/REL/6/4/30; HAS, HD1/5, no. 132210; tithe award, http://www.bosburyhistoryresource.org.uk (accessed 31 Aug. 15).
70 *Domesday*, 502; HAS, AA59/A/1, pp. 156–7, 159; below, Religious Hist.
71 HAS, AA59/A/1, p. 153; HCA 1925. The document is mutilated, the recipient's first name and part of the date being lost.
72 HAS, AA59/A/2, f. 21v.; TNA, E 150/431/4; TNA, C 3/274/44.
73 HAS, Q/REL/6/4/1; HAS, AA63/18, p. 332; TNA, PROB 11/1505, will of John Stedman, 1809. Stedman first occurs in the Bosbury court books in 1786: HAS, AA63/16, pp. 283–4.
74 TNA, PROB 11/656; *London Gaz.* 6 Jul. 1852, 1903.
75 Bentley, *Hist. Bosbury* (1891), 39; Robinson, *Mansions and Manors*, 35.
76 Par. Rec., burials 1884, marriages 1852; *Kelly's Dir. Herefs.* (1885).
77 *The Times*, 27 July 1911, 4, 20.
78 TNA, MAF 48/310; MAF 48/312; MAF 174/109; below Econ. Hist.
79 HAS, AS94/211; *Kelly's Dir. Herefs.* (1941); inf. from Mr. T.N. Hone.

The Grange

The 'heirs of Henry de Stanford' held a second freehold yardland *c.*1280. In 1330 John and Alice de Stanford settled a messuage and yardland, with other property in Bosbury, on John's son John, his wife Margaret and their heirs. In 1578 the estate, called the Grange, was held by James Halfhide or Hawfield, successor of John Halfhide who in 1526 did homage to the bishop for lands held by military service.[80] The later description of the Morton chapel in the parish church as Richard Hawfield's chapel confirms the early 19th century belief that Sir Rowland Morton had earlier lived at, or at least owned, the Grange.[81] By 1594 the Grange had passed to Anthony Hawfield, and in 1625 to Richard Hawfield. The John Hawfield who died in 1676 or 1677 holding free land on the manor was probably one of Anthony's successors.[82] Another Anthony Hawfield died in 1692 and was succeeded by his nephew Thomas Hawfield,[83] but they were not said to have held freehold land. In 1749 Richard Hardwick owned the Grange.[84] A descendant or descendants of the same name owned it in 1789 and a Mrs Hardwick in 1797. By 1802 her tenant, Robert Drew, had acquired the estate, which he still occupied in 1818. In 1848 the farm belonged to Thomas Heywood of Hope End, Colwall.[85] Samuel Willcox acquired it in 1869 and lived there from 1891 or earlier until his death in 1915.[86] The house and *c.*154 a. of land was advertised for sale in 1930.[87]

The third freehold on the bishop's manor in the 1280s was held by Richard son of Mariot, who was followed *c.*1578 by a Powell, possibly the William Powell who held a large customary estate in the manor.[88] The later history of the estate cannot be traced.

Upleadon Manor (Temple Court)

Upleadon had been held before the Conquest by Edith, sister of the Earl Odda who held a west midland earldom. She may in fact have been Odda's tenant; if she was, the Upleadon estate, with those held by Odda directly, would have passed to Edward the Confessor on the earl's death in 1056. The estate may have been the Upledene earlier seized from the church of Worcester by Ranig, an earl of Herefordshire under Cnut. In 1086 it was held by Albert of Lorraine, one of the Confessor's chaplains, who also served William I.[89] By the late 1130s Albert's manor had passed to John Marshal, father

---

80 HAS, AA59/A/1, p. 153; AA59/A/2, f. 21v.; TNA, CP 25/1/82/37, number 20, from http://www.medievalgenealogy.org.uk/fines/abstracts (accessed 10 Apr. 2013); *Reg. Bothe*, 175.

81 TNA, PROB 11/145, will of John Lawrence, 1588; Bentley, *Hist. Bosbury* (1891), 38.

82 HAS, 22/2/32 will of John Hickcox, 1594; HAS, AA63/3, p. 80.

83 HAS, AA63/4, pp. 212, 122; AA63/5, p. 46.

84 Par. Rec., vestry bk. vol. 1, p. 19.

85 HAS, Q/REL/6/4/3, 4, 5, 8, 15, 24; HAS, K19/1.

86 Par. Rec. burials 1915; from http://www.bosburyhistoryresource.org.uk (accessed 28 Aug. 2015); M.G. Watkins continuation of Duncumb's *Herefordshire*, (1902), 29; TNA, RG 12/2051; RG 13/2470; RG 14/15602.

87 HAS, M5/5/35, sale cat.

88 HAS, AA59/A/1, p. 153; AA59/A/2, f. 40v.

89 *Domesday*, 512; A. Williams, *Land, power and politics: the family and career of Odda of Deerhurst* (1996), 2–3. Edith is known only from the Domesday Book entry for Upleadon. For Ranig see http://www.pase.ac.uk (accessed 26 Apr. 2016), and A. Williams, 'The spoliation of Worcester', *Anglo-Norman Studies* 19 (1996), 401, cited in an unpubl. article by B. Coplestone-Crow.

of William Marshal earl of Pembroke.[90] In 1212 Earl William Marshal held Upleadon, 'of his inheritance from the conquest of England', but before his death in 1219 he granted four hides there to the military order of the Knights Templar.[91] William Marshal was succeeded in the earldom of Pembroke by his sons William (d. 1231), Richard (d. 1234), Gilbert (d. 1241), and Walter (d. 1245), all of whom died without heirs.[92] In 1242 the former Marshal estate was divided between the Templar estate, called Upleadon, and Catley held by Isabel of Pembridge of W[alter] Earl Marshal.[93] The overlordship, like the borough and manor of Newbury,[94] presumably should have descended to the Marshal's heirs. It was not specifically recorded again, but in 1338 the Hospitallers paid ½ mark (6s. 8d.) rent to 'divers lords' from their estate of Upleadon. Between 1547 and 1595, courts for Upleadon or Temple Court were held for Edward VI, Mary, and Elizabeth I, possibly as overlords.[95]

The Templars' estates were confiscated by Edward II in 1308. Upleadon was still in the king's hands at the end of 1311, but in 1316 it was held by Thomas earl of Lancaster. On his execution in 1322 his widow, Alice de Lacy, claimed it, and in 1323 the keeper was ordered to hand it over to her, if it was appurtenant to the manor of Clifford (Herefs.), which in 1322 she had sold to the king and received back for her life. Alice presumably forfeited the manor on her second marriage in 1324.[96] By 1338 it, like most of the former Templar lands, had passed to the Hospitallers,[97] who held it until the Dissolution. In 1426 the king seized Upleadon on the grounds that part of it had been given to the Hospitallers to maintain three priests in the manorial chapel and ten sick men (in five beds) and that the current preceptor had failed to do so.[98] If the allegation was true, the land was an addition to the original Upleadon manor granted to the Templars.

In 1544 Hugh ap Harry and his wife Eleanor bought the manor of Upleadon, then occupied by Anthony Washbourne, from the Crown; presumably the purchase was a speculation as the following year they conveyed the manor to John Scudamore (d. 1571), founder of the Holme Lacy branch of the family.[99] Between 1575 and 1579 John's grandson, another John Scudamore, and Ralph Shelton made a series of conveyances of Upleadon, with the manors of Church Lench and Bishampton (Worcs), probably as

90   R.H.C. Davis *(ed.) Regesta Regum Anglo-Normannorum* I, no. 381; E. Mason (ed.) *Westminster Abbey Charters* (London Rec. Soc. 25, 1988), no. 55, cited by Coplestone-Crow.
91   *Book. of Fees*, I. 100; II. 808. He joined the order on his deathbed: *ODNB* s.v. Marshal, William (I) [*called* the Marshal], fourth earl of Pembroke (*c*.1146–1219), soldier and administrator (accessed 3 Jun. 2016).
92   *ODNB*, s.v. Marshal, William (II), fifth earl of Pembroke (*c*.1190–1231) (accessed 3 Jun. 2016).
93   *Book of Fees*, ii, 808.
94   *VCH Berks*. IV, 135.
95   L.B. Larking (ed.), *Knights Hospitallers in England* (Camden Soc. 1857), 195; TNA, SC 2/176/102; TNA, LR 3/21/3; HAS, BF77/13.
96   TNA, SC 8/263/13119; TNA, DL 41/105, item 1; *Feud. Aids*, ii, pp. 388; *Cal. Close 1307–13*, 387–8; 1318–23, 646, 656; 1333–7, 424, cf. Middleton Stoney (Oxon.): *VCH Oxon*. VI, 245. On the Templars see below, Glossary.
97   *Knights Hospitallers in England*, 195.
98   *Cal. Close 1422–9*, 224.
99   *L & P Hen VIII*, XIX (part 1), 171; XX (part 2), 231; for the family see *ODNB* s.v. Scudamore family (*per*. 1500–1820), gentry (accessed 3 Jun. 2016).

part of a settlement.[100] The Worcestershire manors, and so presumably Upleadon, had descended to John not from his grandfather but from his father William Scudamore (d. 1560).[101] The men who made a conveyance of the manor in 1611 and dealt with lands in it between 1613 and 1616 were presumably trustees for the Scudamores.[102]

The second John Scudamore died in 1623 and was succeeded by his grandson, a third John Scudamore, who was created Viscount Scudamore in 1628. In 1635 he conveyed Temple Court to Robert Pye.[103] Pye died in 1662, devising nearly all his lands to his eldest son Robert, who was assessed on £100 worth of land in Upleadon in 1663.[104] Upleadon descended from the second Robert, who died in 1702, to his youngest son Richard;[105] from Richard it passed to his daughter Sarah, wife of William Turton, and to her daughter (d. 1805) and granddaughter (d. 1828), both called Sarah Rowe. The second Sarah devised Upleadon to her distant cousin, Henry Alington of Swinhope, Lincs., who sold it to John Pitt.[106] Pitt, by his will dated 1884, devised Temple Court, which he said had been bought from the devisees of James Barrett, to his son John Harford Pitt and his heirs. John H. Pitt owned it in 1910, and G.H. Pitt of Ledbury in 1941.[107]

Catley

The first William Marshal gave his Catley estate to Stephen Devereux of Lyonshall (d. 1228) whose widow Isabel married Ralph of Pembridge.[108] Henry of Pembridge died in 1279 holding rents of assize in Catley of the gift of William Devereux; he was succeeded by his son Fulk. In 1350 another Fulk de Pembridge died holding an annual rent in Catley of Roger Tyrel and was succeeded by his son, a third Fulk.[109]

In 1651 Humphrey Berrington forfeited lands including the manor of Catley in Bosbury, which he recovered in 1659.[110] The estate may earlier have been held by Thomas Myntriche, who was assessed on land in Upleadon in 1524, for the Berringtons acquired Myntriche land in Stoke Lacy.[111] There is no other record of a Catley manor.

The Brydges Estate

The family was first recorded in Bosbury parish in 1467 when Roger Bridge surrendered copyhold land in Upleadon to the use of his son Richard. In 1505 Richard Bridge held

100 HAS, VCH slips for Bosbury.
101 *VCH Worcs.* III, 46; Robinson, *Mansions and Manors*, 142–3.
102 HAS, A81/II/88, 89, 93
103 HAS, CF50/116, f. 388; *ODNB*, s.v. Scudamore, John, first Viscount Scudamore (1601–71), diplomat and politician (accessed 3 Jun. 2016).
104 TNA, PROB 11/308, will of Robert Pye of Westminster, 1662; M.A. Faraday (ed.), *Hereford Militia Assessments* (Camden, 4th ser. 10, 1972), 102.
105 *VCH Berks.* IV, 490; W.H. Rylands (ed.), *The four visitations of Berkshire made ... 1532; 1566; 1623; 1665–66* (London, 1907), 270, s.v. Pye of Faringdon.
106 http://landedfamilies.blogspot.co.uk/2015/09/182–armstrong-and-heaton-armstrong-of.html (accessed 6 Nov. 2015); HAS, Q/REL/6/4/2; Bentley, *Hist. Bosbury* (1891), 38.
107 HAS, D96/10; TNA, IR 58/38653; TNA, MAF 32/3/147.
108 Unpubl. paper by B. Coplestone-Crow. On the Devereux family see B. Holden, *Lords of the Central Marches* (Oxford, 2008), 97–102.
109 *Cal. Inq. p.m.* II, no. 305, p. 174; *Cal. Inq. p.m.* III, no. 340, p. 209.
110 TNA, C 3/453/77; *Cal. Cttee. for Compounding*, part 3, 2000.
111 Faraday (ed.), *Herefs. Taxes in the Reign of Henry VIII*, 68; Robinson, *Mansions and Manors*, 260.

three messuages and 2 yardlands there. In 1560 customary lands in Upleadon were
settled on Anne, widow of another Richard Bridge, for her life with remainder to James
Bridge the younger and his wife Jane. James Bridge of Upleadon held land of Upleadon
manor in 1587, as did another James Bridge, of Catley.[112] In 1613 William Brydges of
Upleadon bought three messuages and 1½ yardlands in the manor of Upleadon. His son
of the same name, who settled at Tibberton in Madley, acquired further copyholds in
1639 and in 1640 or 1641.[113] The marriage settlement in 1680 for his grandson, Francis
Brydges, included a capital messuage called Upleadon, probably on the site of the later
Upleadon Court, and Nelmes, the Farm, Noverend (in Bosbury), New Court, and a
messuage in Staplow, as well as land in Stanley hill and five other unnamed tenements
in Bosbury.[114] The estate descended to Francis's great grandson, Francis William Thomas
Brydges (d. 1793), who was assessed on a total of £17–worth of land in Upleadon in
1786, then to his daughter Ann and her husband Henry Lee Warner.[115] In 1807 at least
part of the estate, including Upleadon Court, belonged to George Mayo, who passed it to
his nephew, George Shayle. On Shayle's death in 1881 the estate was divided between his
daughters Ada Shayle and Elizabeth Mayo Hawkins.[116]

Francis Brydges of Hereford bought land in Upleadon in 1698 and 1707, and a
Richard Brydges owned Lower Townend in Bosbury in 1775.[117]

Local Government

Manorial Courts

Both the bishops of Hereford in Bosbury and the Templars and Hospitallers in Upleadon
held courts for their manors. The bishop's rights in all his manors were confirmed by
Henry I between 1115 and 1121, the Templars' by Richard I in 1189.[118] In 1292 the bishop
claimed extensive rights including view of frankpledge and the assizes of bread and of ale,
and the right to hear pleas of the crown in his manors.[119] Surviving compotuses record
receipts from perquisites of court on the bishop's manor from 1294; on the Templars'
manor from c.1308.[120]

The bishops' courts from the late 15th to the early 17th century, although mainly
concerned with agricultural matters, including stray animals, and the conveyance of
copyholds, dealt with cases of affray and bloodshed, and with breaches of the assizes of

112 HAS, BF77/12, 13; HAS, A63/III/23/1, f. 9v.; TNA, LR 3/21/3.
113 HAS, A81/II/89, 90, 95; Robinson, *Mansions and Manors*, 268; John Burke, *Hist. Landed Gentry or Commoners of Great Britain and Ireland* (1838), 552.
114 HAS, A81/II/2. His great-grandson, Francis William Thomas Brydges, owned the site of Upleadon Court but not that of the modern Upleadon Farm: HAS, AS80/5.
115 HAS, Q/REL /6/2/2; HAS, cat. of A81.
116 HAS, D96/9.
117 HAS, A81/II/99, 100; HAS, D96/89.
118 *Charters and Records of Hereford Cathedral*, ed. W.W. Capes, 3; *Cartae Antiquae* (PRS, n.s. 33), no. 588.
119 *Placita de Quo Warranto* (Rec. Com.), 270.
120 HCA, R366; TNA, E 199/18/4.

bread and of ale.[121] A court in 1619 accused the inhabitants of failing to practise with the long bow in accordance with the statute; one in 1622 ordered an investigation into the state of the bridge in Bosbury village and the road across it to Upleadon.[122] Business in 16th-century courts for Upleadon manor was similar, including pleas of debt, affray, and bloodshed; in 1547 a man and a woman disturbed the court with 'a tumult and talking'. In 1548 Thomas Farley was ordered to remove his female servant who was 'of ill fame and conversation'. Numerous orders were made for tenants to repair roads and scour ditches.[123] On both manors courts with view of frankpledge were held twice a year, in spring and autumn; presumably other courts were held more frequently, but no records survive for Bosbury manor until 1715 when courts baron for Bosbury (concerned almost entirely with the transfer of copyholds) began to be entered into the bishop's court books.[124] There are records of courts baron for Upleadon manor in 1587, 1591, and 1592, but no later records of any Upleadon manorial courts survive.[125]

Among the customs recorded in 1674 for the bishop's manors of Bosbury, Colwall and Coddington was that copyholds should descend to the son or eldest daughter of the copyholder; a widow should hold in free bench for life, provided her husband left no children by a former marriage. Copyholders were exempt from service at the assizes or sessions of the peace, from appearing before the clerk of the market, or paying toll at any market within the diocese.[126]

From 1661, when the surviving series of court books begins, the business of the bishop's court was increasingly confined to the conveyance of copyholds. Until the early 18th century courts continued to order the repair of houses, roads, bridges, and watercourses; they also ordered the ringing of pigs, and forbade the taking of 'inmates' or lodgers. In 1674 the jurors reported that there were no archery butts on the manor. In the same year the pound lacked a lock, and the next year it was 'decayed'.[127] The court met twice a year until 1875, then once a year until the last court baron was held in June 1885. The last records for court business, transacted out of court, are from 1943. The copyhold lands of the bishop's manor started to be enfranchised from 1855 and such enfranchisements become more frequent from 1860.[128]

Constables were appointed in the bishop's court from 1619, and in Upleadon court in 1587.[129] A bailiff and a hayward (an officer in charge of the common land) were appointed in the court in 1827 and a hayward in 1830.[130]

121 HAS, AM33/1, 2, 6, 8, 9.
122 HAS, AM33/8
123 TNA, SC 2/176/102; TNA, LR 3/21/3.
124 HAS, AA63/8, p. 86.
125 TNA, LR 3/21/3; TNA, SC 2/176/103.
126 HAS, AA26/I/5.
127 HAS, AA63/2, pp. 270, 285, 309.
128 HAS, AA63/1–AA63/38.
129 HAS, AM33/8; TNA, LR 3/21/3.
130 HAS, AA63/25, p. 160; AA63/26 p. 242.

Parochial Government

The vestry minutes, which survive from 1741, record the appointment of parish officers, including churchwardens and overseers of the poor. By 1754 one churchwarden was selected by the vicar and one elected by the parishioners; in 1853 one churchwarden was elected for Bosbury and one for Upleadon. Separate overseers were appointed for Bosbury and Upleadon; their numbers varied, three for each side (or division) of the parish being chosen in 1757 and 1758, only one overseer for each division in 1824, but as many as four for each division in 1838, and three in 1853. A petty constable was first appointed in 1764, and a surveyor of highways in 1765.[131] An inspector of nuisances was appointed in 1857 but the post only lasted until 1859 when the role was subsumed into the work of the surveyors of the highways. In 1853 there were separate surveyors for each of the three divisions of Bosbury, Upleadon and Catley. There were also two guardians and eight constables.[132] In 1863 a waywarden was appointed in each of the three divisions to oversee its roads. Overseers of the poor were last appointed in 1894.[133]

The vestry met in the church for the majority of meetings although in 1776 it was decided that 'parish meetings' were to be held alternately at the Crown and the Bell inns. Although in 1817 it was resolved to erect a vestry in the north-west corner of the church, there is no clear evidence that this was done. From 1849 most meetings were held in the boys' school.[134]

Bosbury was in Ledbury Poor Law Union from 1834 and the Ledbury Rural District from 1894 until the union of Herefordshire and Worcestershire in 1974.[135] It then became part of Malvern Hills District until 1998 when the parish became part of Hope End Ward in the Herefordshire Unitary Authority.[136] In the 1990s the parish merged with Coddington to form Bosbury and Coddington parish.

---

131 Par. Rec., vestry mins. vol. 1 pp. 107–8.
132 Par. Rec., vestry mins. vol. 4, Easter Monday 1853. The number of constables varied from year to year, e.g. four in 1858 and six in 1859.
133 Par. Rec., vestry mins. vol. 4, meetings of 30 Mar. 1863, 22 Mar. 1894.
134 Par. Rec., vestry mins. passim.
135 Youngs, *Admin. Units* II, 671; http://www.visionofbritain.org.uk/unit/10190307 (accessed 16 Sept. 2015).
136 http://www.legislation.gov.uk/uksi/1996/1867/schedule/3/made (accessed 20 Apr. 2016).

ECONOMIC HISTORY

Agriculture

Medieval and Early Modern Agriculture

THE TOTAL OF 59 PLOUGHS, two on each demesne and the rest on the tenants' land, recorded in Bosbury and Upleadon in 1086, suggests that the parish was already intensively cultivated as arable, even though a third plough might have been employed on the Upleadon demesne.[1] The amount of arable, at least on the bishop's demesne, seems to have remained the same at least until the early 15th century: in 1240 when Peter de Aigueblanche became bishop of Hereford there were 12 oxen and one draught animal on his Bosbury manor, and in 1291 and 1404 two ploughlands of demesne were reported there.[2] The bishop's rental of c.1288 recorded 423½ a. of arable in the demesne. In 1293–4 the reeve accounted for sowing 125½ a. with wheat, 102 ½ a. with oats, and 3 a. with peas on the demesne, suggesting that the three-course rotation usual in the area was followed in Bosbury: land being sown mainly with wheat one year, with oats and some peas the next, and left fallow in the third year.[3] Tenants on the bishop's manor still owed unspecified works in the later 14th century.[4]

On Upleadon manor c.1308, the keeper of the manor paid for ploughing 81 a. for the summer sowing, 81 a. for the fallow, and 83 a. in the winter, but he paid for harvesting 360 a. of grain.[5] Presumably some of the ploughing was done by labour services: c.1322 the yardlanders on the manor owed ploughing, sowing and harrowing works. At least one tenant owed two harvest works in 1505.[6]

In 1505 Upleadon manor house and the demesne adjoining it was leased to Thomas Leyland; he and nine other tenants leased parts of the demesne ranging in size from 19 a. to 2 a., all apparently intermixed with customary and freehold land, as well as unspecified parcels and the whole of a field called Shilley field; Shilley field was still being leased in the 1540s.[7] By the early 16th century the bishops were also leasing their demesne, 40 a. in

1   *Domesday*, 502, 512.
2   *English Episcopal Acta*, vii, *Hereford 1234–75*, no. 87n.; *Taxatio Ecclesiastica* (Rec. Com.), 168; *Cal. Inq. Misc.* vii, no. 281.
3   HAS, AA59/A/1, p. 155; HCA, R366.
4   TNA, SC 6/1138/5. For the rotation see A.J. Roderick, 'Open-field agriculture in Herefordshire in the later Middle Ages', *TWNFC*, 33 (1949), 55–7.
5   TNA, E 199/18/4; TNA, E 358/18 from notes supplied by Prof. Helen Nicholson.
6   TNA, SC 6/860/19; HAS, A63/III/23/1, f. 8v.
7   HAS, A63/II/23/1, ff. 7v.–10v.; TNA, SC 2/176/102, courts on 4 Oct. 1 Edw. VI, 2 Apr. 4 Edw. VI.

Pangons Hill or 'Held' to a single tenant, in addition to leasing the bulk of the demesne to Thomas Morton.[8]

Common Fields

Until well into the 18th century much of Bosbury parish was covered by common fields in which different owners or tenants held strips. These were marked out by the ridge and furrow which in 2015 survived only in the pasture field formerly called Harlands Wood, east-south-east of Bosbury village. All the strips in a field were ploughed and harvested at the same time, and livestock were allowed onto the fields after harvest and during the fallow year. Although a three-course rotation was followed, there is no evidence at Bosbury for the three field system, or division of the arable into three large fields or groups of fields, which seems to have obtained further west and north in the Wye and Lugg valleys.[9]

The survey of the bishop's manor in 1578, which covered the demesne and customary (but not the freehold) lands of the manor,[10] described a total of 1,312 a., including house sites, of which 478½ a. of arable were unevenly distributed among 20 common fields, most of which also contained inclosed land. By far the largest field was South field (128 a.) which covered the area to the south of Bosbury village, between the Leadon and the parish boundary. It contained both demesne and customary land, but the demesne land, most of which lay in large blocks, had been consolidated if not inclosed. South field was the only field which seems to have been subdivided in any way: 12 a. of land there lay in Raddenhill and Ruddale or Rudhall. Court field (53 a.) immediately south of the village was almost entirely made up of demesne and forlet land, with 9 a. belonging to the rectory and 1½ a. of customary land. Bacon (later Beacon) Hill field on the northern parish boundary contained 15 a. of demesne and forlet land to 4 a. of customary land. The smallest field, Strowd Hill (6 a.) probably near Beacon hill, was entirely composed of forlet land, and Arbour Hill (10 a.), north of the village contained 8 a. of forlet land. Many other small fields or closes contained a few acres of forlet land. The second largest field, Winsordine (57 a.) lay north-east of the village, towards the parish boundary; it contained only customary land, as did the other larger fields: Lyefield (38 a., west of Nashend), Windmill Hill (24 a., probably due east of the village), Hanley (22½ a., possibly the tithe award Houndley field near the eastern boundary of the parish between Slatch Farm and the Moat) and Long Acre field (19½ a. north of the village on the eastern bank of the Leadon). The remaining fields, which varied in size from 18 a. down to 6 a., were similarly composed of customary land; those which can be identified lay north and slightly east of the village.

No tenant in 1578 held land in all the common fields. John Allen, whose 82-a. holding was one of the larger ones on the manor, held land in 11 fields, including both South and Winsordine fields; John Brown's 70-a. holding and William Powell's 52½ a. were each divided between only two fields: Winsordine field and Lye field. Only two tenants, James Barnes (53½ a.) and John Leeth (36 a.) did not have any land in

8   TNA, SC 6/HenVIII/1511. Pangons hill has not been identified.
9   See H.L. Gray, *English Field Systems* (1915, reprinted 1959), 37, 93, 142–4; W.E. Tate, 'Hand list of enclosure awards', *TWNFC* (1941), 183–90.
10   HAS, AA59/A/2, ff. 1–54v. Identifications of fields from the tithe map as redrawn by Geoff Gwatkin. For forlet land (probably former demesne) see below, Glossary.

Figure 7 *Detail of opening page of survey of the bishop of Hereford's Bosbury estate 1577–8. The title
'Bosbury' appears between the flowers at the top of the page; the Latin for 'Court Baron and View [of
frankpledge]' below.*

Winsordine field; five tenants, including Barnes and Leeth, had no land in South field.
There were presumably several different groupings of fields for cultivation on the three-
course rotation described above.

The Upleadon rental of 1505 recorded land in four areas called fields: South field,
Williams field, Birchernes field and Le Shilley, the last apparently composed of demesne
land. South field contained areas called 'doles' of 2–3 a. Three other 'fields' appear to have
been closes held by one tenant. Other areas including Staplow, Ashcroft, Barland, and
Lyneacre (later Linegar) were also common fields. The smallest holding was 1 a., and
only one holding (12 a. of free land) was specifically described as 'lying divided in the
field'; others may well have been consolidated. The acres were usually held in addition
to yardlands and half yardlands, which were not described in detail.[11] South field may
have been Catleys Suffield recorded in 1547.[12] By the 17th century there were nine or
ten common fields in Upleadon. In 1634 a holding there contained 24 a. in six common
fields: Hemma, Upleadons Southfield, Barland, Linnacre, Diddadine and Inchcroft; half
of those acres were in Barland. Barland or Bareland was also recorded in 1631 when an
Upleadon man bequeathed 3 a. of arable there, as well as 1 a. in Ashcroft, and 2 a. in the

11   HAS, A63/III/23/1, ff. 7.–10v.
12   TNA, SC 2/176/102, court 4 Oct. 1 Edw. VI.

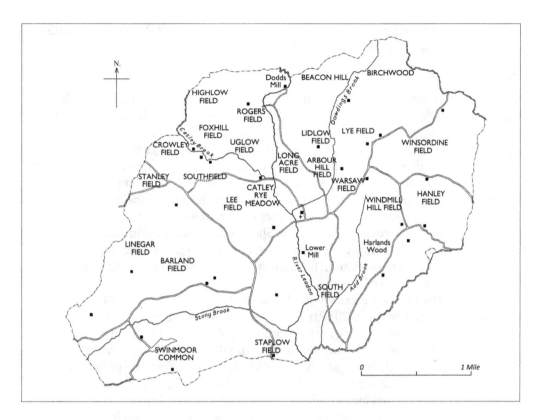

Map 3 *Bosbury common fields c.1840.*

Lea, which was recorded in 1666 as a common field. In 1649 nine ridges in Fox Hill field (in Catley) and 10 ridges and ½ a. in Flea Hill field in Upleadon manor were the subject of a conveyance. Ten a. of land in Moor End Ley were recorded in 1671, and in 1707 18 a. lay scattered in a common field called Moor End Ley on the boundary with Munsley. In 1673 a yeoman held 3 a. in a common field called Stapley (Staplow).[13] As on Bosbury manor, it is not clear how these fields were organised for cultivation.

The tithe award in 1839 recorded ten 'common fields' in Bosbury parish: Crowley, Foxhill (or Foxhall), Highlow or Hilow, Lee, Lidlow, Linegar, Common Southfield, Stanley, Uglow and Winsordine. Of these Crowley, Foxhill, Highlow, Common Southfield, and Uglow were in Catley where an area called Rogers Field and Rogers Hill also contained common field strips. Lee and Stanley were in Upleadon, on the border with Catley. Linegar field was on the western parish boundary, with Canon Frome. Great, Little and Upper Staplow fields on the southern edge of Upleadon also contained unenclosed strips, although they were not described as common fields. As well as Lidlow and Winsordine common fields, Warsaw field on Bosbury manor was still largely

13   HAS, K12/4; HAS, A81/II/96, 100; HAS, AH83/11; HAS, 41/1/1, will of Michael Lawrence 1631;
      12/1/32, will of Richard Lawrence, 1666; 122/5/14, will of Richard Baker (dated 1673, proved 1697).

unenclosed. Seven common fields, all in Catley, survived until 1854: Lee, Rogers Hill, Rogers Field, Catley South Field, Fox Hill, Uglow, Highlow, and Crowley.[14]

Crops and Livestock

About 1288 the customary tenants on the bishop's manor had to sow part of the demesne with their own wheat and oats.[15] In 1293–4 a total of 134 loads of wheat, 52 loads of oats, and 20½ loads of peas were grown on the bishop's demesne. In addition, at least 75 loads of dredge (a mixture of barley and oats) were used, mainly as wages for four ploughmen, two carters, and a dairyman. Remarkably, the reeve accounted for up to 20 peacocks and peahens, and six swans, as well as geese and hens, and an unspecified number of doves in the dovecote. The peacocks in particular indicate the high status of the manor as one of Bishop Swinfield's favourite residences. Four of the swans were sent to the kitchen, but it is not clear what the peacocks were used for. Sheep were mentioned in connection with mowing a meadow. The presence of a dairyman implies cows, but none were specifically recorded. The number of oxen, used for ploughing, fluctuated between 20 and 24 over the year. Bees were also kept.[16]

Wheat was the main crop grown on Upleadon manor in 1308 and 1309, with 138 qtr grown in the first year and 201 qtr in the second, followed by oats (109½ qtr and 154 qtr) and peas (22 qtr and 16½ qtr); in 1308 almost as much maslin (rye mixed with wheat) (103 qtr) as oats was grown, but no maslin was grown in 1309. Wheat from the manor was sent to Hereford and Monmouth for sale. Apples were grown to make cider, four casks of which were sold in 1308. The livestock in 1308 consisted of 5 horses and a foal, 38 oxen, 9 cows and a bull, 8 bullocks and 7 calves, 1 boar and 45 pigs; milk from the cows was sold. The carcasses of four sheep were sold, but no live animals were recorded although there presumably was a flock. In 1308 there were also 12 geese and 9 ganders.[17] The place-name Vineyard or Vynours recorded in 1505 suggests earlier vine-growing on Upleadon manor. The bishop's manorial court dealt with stray sheep in 1476 and *c.*1556.[18]

The wills and inventories of the 16th and 17th centuries confirm the impression that land in Bosbury was mainly cultivated as arable. Wheat, rye, muncorn (mixed grain), barley, and oats were regularly recorded from the 16th century, as well as peas (a fodder crop?).[19] One man in 1610 left hops; one in 1612 had hemp (for making cloth), another in 1627 'hemp or flax'.[20] Flax was not recorded again until 1694 when John Allcott had both woollen yarn and flax.[21] The later 17th-century evidence suggests that a three-course

14   HAS, M5/44/9 (tithe map), redrawn by Geoff Gwatkin; HAS, Q/RI/4.
15   HAS, AA59/A/1, p. 158.
16   HCA, R366.
17   TNA, E 199/18/4; TNA, E 358/18, from notes kindly supplied by Prof. Helen Nicholson. There are slight discrepancies between the rolls on the number of livestock.
18   HAS, A63/III/23/1, f. 8; HAS, AM33/1, court of 6 Oct. 1476; AM33/6, court (date lost) 1555–6.
19   e.g. HAS, 32/1/1, will of Nicholas ap Powell, 1544; 27/1/36, will of John Lawrence, 1588; 45/1/49, will of William ap Harry, 1595; 21/2/36, will of Thomas Hall, 1571; 9/3/81, will of James Bridge, 1598.
20   HAS, 18/4/5, will of Richard Wooding, 1610; 16/4/17, will of Richard Finch, 1613; TNA, PROB 11/152, will of William Bridge, 1627.
21   HAS, 117/4/23, will of John Allcott, 1694.

rotation of winter wheat, spring sown crops and a fallow was still followed.[22] In March 1672 William Powell left Lent grain, presumably harvested the previous autumn, threshed in his house, and 9 a. of white corn and 29 a. of peas and pulse growing on his land. In the summer of 1673 Henry Smallridge had 15 a. of corn and barley to 23 a. of pulse and peas, but John Bowen had 10 a. each of corn and barley and pulses and beans.[23] In November 1679 John Danett apparently had 52 a. of corn and barley and 52 a. of peas, but in November 1682 Elizabeth Mutlow had only wheat, rye and muncorn growing although she had peas and pulse, as well as other grain harvested and stored in her barns.[24] In January 1694 Francis Hill left peas, pulse and corn in his barn, but only corn growing on the ground, implying that peas and pulse were a spring-sown crop. In 1613 a ridge of hemp was to be sown each year for three years, presumably not the same ridge each year.[25]

A stray ram was presented at Upleadon in 1547.[26] Many 17th-century testators had kept a few cattle, including plough oxen and bullocks. Several of these cattle had names, like the ox called Pheasant in 1555, and the cow called Rose in 1631. The largest herd recorded was the 18 cows owned by John Danett in 1679, followed by the 10 owned by Henry Smallridge in 1673.[27] A few people kept sheep, usually fewer than 10, but James Woodyatt in 1598 had 37, Henry Bray in 1664 had 81, and John Danett in 1679 had 115; Henry Milward in 1675 had Welsh sheep.[28] Three men, in 1594, 1619 and 1658 kept bees.[29]

Meadow and Pasture

Only 8 a. of meadow, on Bosbury manor, was recorded in the parish in 1086, but the numerous streams must always have watered extensive meadows. By c.1360 there were 33 a. of meadow on the bishop's demesne alone. The survey of 1578 recorded a total of c.55 a. of meadow and over 147 a. of pasture on the manor. Almost all holdings then included a few acres of either meadow or pasture.[30]

On Upleadon manor in 1309 there were 20 a. of hay meadow on the demesne, and by 1338 there were 40 a. of meadow on the manor as a whole.[31] Catley Rye meadow was common pasture in 1587 when a tenant of the manor was accused of grazing many more cattle there than the stint laid down by the manorial court; the following year one man had one cow too many on the meadow.[32] By 1698 a total of 3¼ a. of arable beside the Leadon in Upleadon had been converted from arable to meadow or pasture. A total of 22

---

22 HAS, 41/1/1, will of Michael Lawrence, 1631; 30/3/25, will of Thomas Knight, 1671.
23 HAS, 35/5/19, will of William Powell, 1672; 37/2/25, will of Henry Smallridge, 1673; 37/3/8, will of John Bowen, 1673.
24 HAS, 63/1/5, will of John Danett, 1679; 77/3/11, will of Elizabeth Mutlow, 1682.
25 HAS, 118/2/3, will of Francis Hill, 1694; 16/4/17, will of Richard Finch the elder,1613.
26 TNA, SC 2/176/102, court 4 Oct. 1 Edw. VI.
27 HAS, 31/2/14, will of William Mutlow, 1555; 41/1/1, will of Michael Lawrence, 1631; 37/2/25, will of Henry Smallridge, 1673; 63/1/5, will of John Danett, 1679.
28 HAS, 45/4/76, will of James Woodyatt, 1598; 4/3/4, will of Henry Bray, 1664; 63/1/5, will of John Danett, 1679; 44/1/12, will of Henry Millward, 1675.
29 HAS, 7/2/32, will of Richard Baker, 1594; 27/1/35; will of William Shewell, 1619; 1/5/8, will of Anthony Huck, 1658.
30 *Domesday*, 502; TNA, SC 6/1138/5; HAS, AA59/A/2, ff. 1–32.
31 TNA, E 199/18/4; *Knights Hospitallers in England*, ed. L.B. Larking (Camd. Soc., 1857), 195.
32 TNA, LR 3/21/3, courts on 18 Oct. 29 Eliz. I, 3 Oct. 30 Eliz. I.

a. of grass in Catley Rye meadow was inclosed by Act of Parliament in 1854, and 7 a. of grass in Swinmore Common in 1865.[33]

Woodland

A wood on the bishop's manor in 1086 rendered nothing. About 1288 the bishop's customary tenants were allowed four loads of firewood a year each from the bishop's wood.[34] Both these references were probably to Birchwood in the north-east quarter of the parish, where in 1293–4 the bishop's customary tenants had pannage for their pigs. The fact that money was spent 'enclosing' it, presumably to protect young shoots, suggests that the wood was coppiced.[35] Pasture in Birchwood brought in 12*d.* in 1496–7, and the wood itself was let for 2*s.* a year in the early 16th century.[36] In 1578 the jurors at the bishop's court complained that 28 a. of pasture in Birchwood, extending from the Cradley boundary to the road to Nashend, had been illegally inclosed.[37] Birchwood was still described as a wood in 1759 and 1789; it may have included the demesne coppices at or near Beacon Hill which were leased in 1795.[38]

In 1577 a tenant had licence to cut down coppice wood in Fewell wood, probably near Townend. Other tenants in 1578 held small areas of woodland at, on, or near Beacon Hill (fewer than 10 a.), and at Norbridge in the north-east of the parish by the Cradley road (*c.*3 a.).[39] Tenants held parcels of woodland at Black Venns south of Birchwood in 1703.[40] A total of 9 a. of woodland, in two parcels, and a 10-a. coppice called Monnington's grove, all apparently near Slatch farm in the east of the parish, were conveyed in 1733 with other land in Bosbury and Coddington. Coppice wood (4 a.) near Winsordine field was conveyed in 1740 and 1758.[41]

No wood was recorded on Upleadon manor in 1086, but the place-name Catley, 'cat's wood', recorded from 1243,[42] indicates that that part of the manor was wooded. In 1309 coppice wood from the demesne land was sold. A tenant's wood between Stanley [hill] and Castle Frome was illicitly felled in 1547.[43]

An agreement for the felling of wood in Noverings Coppice made in 1721 allowed the purchaser to fell 260 lugs (or square perches) of wood, leaving three 'poules or standils', presumably standards, of oak or ash in each lug; he was to inclose the coppice with a good hedge and not to dig any sawpits or make charcoal within the coppice.[44]

A 40-a. field south-east of the village, called Harlands Wood in 1839, was described as woodland or pasture in 1795. There is no earlier record of the field, which was on the bishop's demesne, but the well-preserved ridge and furrow indicates that the whole field

33   HAS, A81/II/99; HAS, Q/RI/4, 5.
34   *Domesday*, 502; HAS, AA59/A/1, p. 158.
35   HCA, R366.
36   HAS, AM33/13; HAS, O43.
37   HAS, AA59/A/2, f. 28.
38   HAS, AH83/19; HAS, HD1/4, nos 132170, 132188.
39   HAS, AA59/A/2, ff. 2, 27v., 29v., 41v., 43, 54.
40   HAS, AA63/6, p. 74.
41   HAS, AA63/11, pp. 19, 242; AA63/14, p. 192.
42   Coplestone-Crow, *Herefordshire Place-names* (2009 edn.), 49.
43   TNA, E 358/18, from notes supplied by Prof. Helen Nicholson; TNA, SC 2//176/102, court 4 Oct. 1 Edw. VI.
44   HAS, BF77/14.

had been arable before the eastern part of it was inclosed and planted with trees. In 1839 the whole area was grass.[45]

By 1839 only *c.*150 a. of woodland, mainly coppice, remained in the parish, c.13 a. in plantations. The largest area of woodland (*c.*40 a.) was at Beacon Hill with smaller woods near Bosbury House and in the north-east of the parish. Many farms contained small coppices or plantations, some of which produced the timber 'fit for naval and other purposes' advertised for sale in 1800 and 1808.[46] The Bosbury House estate, which extended onto Beacon Hill was still 'exceptionally well timbered' in 1938,[47] and the wood there survived in 2015. In 1994 New Hill wood (10 a.), in the north-west corner of the parish, was acquired by a group of local woodworkers who renamed it Clissett wood after the 19th-century furniture-maker and formed a Trust to preserve the wood and foster woodworking crafts.[48]

Inclosure

By the early 16th century the holders of some strips or groups of strips in the common fields had inclosed their land, freeing them from the obligation to follow the crop rotation of the field and from the obligation to allow livestock onto the fields after harvest. This inclosure presumably took place by agreement between landholders and resulted in a landscape of scattered inclosures within the common fields.

In 1505 an Upleadon tenant was responsible for maintaining the inclosing hedges at his yardland called Newesland, and another tenant had 12 a. 'lying together severally' called Collhavel, which was a close in 1588.[49] A badly kept hedge inclosing the Old Croft was presented at the Upleadon manor court in 1547, as were other hedges at Stanley, Great Crowley and Little Crowley which may also have surrounded inclosures.[50] The exchange in 1588 of 11 selions (strips) in Dyderdon (probably Diddadine) and Linegar fields for another 11 selions in the same fields for the holders' lives was presumably made to consolidate holdings. An exchange of two holdings of 2½ a. in Linegar in 1589 seems to have been permanent and may have been a prelude to inclosure.[51]

By 1578 nearly 500 a., about half the arable, had been inclosed on the bishop's manor. Most houses were surrounded by inclosures of arable and pasture, some extending to 20 a. or more. Other closes lay intermingled with land in the common fields and seem from their small size, half to three quarters of an acre, to be inclosed strips.[52] Parcels of inclosed land were included in conveyances throughout the 17th and 18th centuries, all the result of private agreements, as no major inclosure agreements are recorded. Land inclosed from Winsordine field was bounded by a ditch in 1703. Three acres lately

45   Geoff Gwatkin, 'Bosbury Tithe Map'; HAS, HD1/4, no. 132170; Keith Ray, unpubl. interim report on excavations in 2015.
46   HAS, microfilm of TNA, IR 29/14, tithe apportionment; *Glouc. Jnl*, 24 Mar. 1800; *Hereford Jnl*, 2 Mar. 1808, both http://www.bosburyhistoryresource.org.uk (accessed 4 May 2016).
47   HAS, M5/5/37 (sale cat.)
48   http://www.greenwoodwork.co.uk/website/clissettwood.html (accessed 5 May 2016).
49   HAS, A63/III/23/1, ff. 8v, 10; TNA, LR 3/21/3, court on 11 Apr. 30 Eliz. I.
50   TNA, SC 2/176/102, court on 22 Apr. I Edw. VI.
51   TNA, LR 3/21/3, courts on 11 Apr. 30 Eliz. I, 30 Apr. 31 Eliz. I.
52   HAS, AA59/A/2

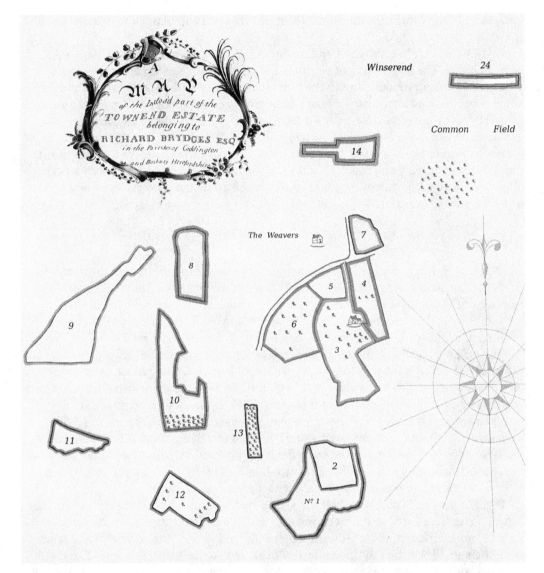

Figure 8 *Part of a map of the Townend Estate, 1775, showing the inclosures in and near Winsordine common field. Those numbered 2, 6, 8, and 10 were arable; 1, 3, 5, 11, 12, 13 and 14 were pasture; 7 and 9 meadow, and 4 hops.*

inclosed from Long Acre field were conveyed in 1714. Two separate acres inclosed out of Winsordine field had been planted with fruit trees by 1747, as had 1½ a. taken from Harbour Hill before 1769. A parcel of arable inclosed out of Long Acre was conveyed in 1780.[53]

Despite these inclosures, in 1801 between a third and a half of the arable in the parish was still farmed in common fields, a situation which the vicar, John Lodge, described

53   HAS, AA63/6, p. 50; AA63/8, p. 82; AA63/12, p. 167; AA63/16, p. 47; AA 63/17, p. 362.

as 'very injurious to general cultivation' because land was left fallow every third year.[54] Presumably piecemeal inclosure by agreement continued in the first half of the 19th century. In 1854 a total of 80 a. of common field arable, all in Upleadon, was inclosed by an award made under the Act of 1845. It was not until 1871 that the few remaining acres lying intermixed in 'Woozer', 'Romney', and Lidlow fields were consolidated by exchange between the owners, including the Church Commissioners and the trustees of the Grammar School.[55] This late inclosure in Upleadon may have been at least partly due to the absence of any dominant landowner in the township.

18th- to 21st-century agriculture

Pasture and Livestock

Fattening cattle for markets in the home counties was an important element in Herefordshire's prosperity between the 17th and the early 19th century.[56] His farm book reveals that in the 1740s Charles Bennett of Temple Court was purchasing cattle from Welsh farmers at fairs in Brampton Bryan in Herefordshire, and at Clun and Bishop's Castle in Shropshire (both c.45 miles from Bosbury). He appears to have grazed the animals on his land for a short period, then sold them on at local markets to dealers, presumably from London and the South Midlands. On one occasion he took cattle in on 'tack' (temporary grazing) for a dealer from Quatford in Shropshire.[57] Bennett's activities were presumably sustained by good pasture and improved meadows, such the 26 a. of meadow ground at Old Court conveyed by William and Anne Bodenham to Bereton Bourchier and John Beard in 1708, with the 'liberty to convey and direct water out of the south part of the Court Field into the park meadow'.[58] This clearly describes a facility for 'drowning', which was carried out in the late winter and could double the grass crop from a meadow. Extensive meadows at Old Court, recorded in a survey of 1795, included the 'Hams' - a traditional name for a natural water meadow. An indenture of 1828 prohibited the tenant from ploughing up meadow or pasture without the landlord's permission. A little earlier another document referred to pasture 'suitable for all manner of cattle' and when its occupier's effects were sold in 1859 Old Court still had 80 head of Hereford pure-bred cattle.[59] Sale catalogues for other properties in the late 19th century and later make few references to meadows or pasture and a reference to meadows of 'feeding quality and well-watered' at Cold Green in 1890 is unusual.[60] The feeding and fattening of cattle in Bosbury appears to have all but died out in the late 19th century. Between 1924 and 1945 75 a. of land at the Nelmes were converted from pasture to arable.[61]

---

54   *Home Office Acreage Returns* (HO 67) (List and Index Soc. 189, 1982), 197–8; J. P. Dodd, 'Herefordshire agriculture in the mid 19th century', *TWNFC*, 43 (1980), 216.

55   HAS, Q/RI/4; HAS, CJ22/1: copy of order of the Enclosure Commissioners 21 July 1871.

56   *Cambridge Agrarian History of England and Wales* IV (1967), ed. J.Thirsk, 102; J. Duncumb, *A General View of the Agriculture of the County of Hereford* (1802), 68, 73–4, 116.

57   HAS, AS94/101; for the Welsh cattle fairs see *Cambridge Agrarian History*, ed. Thirsk, 120–3.

58   HAS, HD1/5, no. 132214.

59   HAS, D96/86; HAS, AS94/288; HAS, AD1/6, Box 2; *Hereford Jnl*, 19 Oct. 1859.

60   HAS, AS94/212.

61   HAS, M5/5/32; M5/5/33 sale cat. 1924 and 1945.

Hops and Orchards

Hops were first recorded in the parish in 1610, and in 1667 the gentleman William Went left hop poles in his hopyard.[62] Hopyards, or hopcrofts, were frequently recorded on farms from 1670.[63] In the 18th century several farm buildings, including part of the gatehouse at Old Court and part of the Dog farmhouse, were adapted for hop-drying.[64] Nineteenth-century hop kilns survive at nine farms, including two at Little Catley.[65] In 1740 Charles Bennett at Temple Court was taking his hops to Worcester.[66] Hop poles from the coppiced woods in the parish were regularly advertised for sale in the columns of the *Hereford Times* in the mid 19th century.[67] Hops were labour intensive and needed tending all the year, providing work for the poor, but also employing migrant workers, including in the late 18th century women from South Wales whose husbands were employed bringing in the declining grain harvest.[68] Bosbury benefitted from its proximity to Worcester, which developed the most flourishing hop-market in the West Midlands, completely eclipsing Hereford by the end of the 18th century.[69] Apart from a brief depression during the Napoleonic Wars, hops continued to flourish during the 19th century, the local newspapers showing deep interest in the health and productivity of this vulnerable crop. Even the stealing of hop-poles for winter fuel was recorded.[70] In 1934 Bosbury was described as a cider and hop district, and in 1938 buildings at Cold Green farm included three blocks of galvanized iron hop-pickers' barracks.[71] In the 2010s hops were still grown in the parish, with one of the national growers' groups, Hawkbrand Hops Ltd, being based there.[72]

Orcharding too has a long history in east Herefordshire. Cider or must mills were frequently mentioned in 16th-century wills.[73] Apples, presumably for cider, were recorded in 1658, and apples and pears for cider and perry, in 1665.[74] The hard Barland pear, recorded from 1658, which was named for Barlands field in Upleadon, was said to make particularly good perry.[75] In 1740 Charles Bennett of Temple Court took cider to Upton-on-Severn (Worcs.),[76] presumably for transport further afield. In the late 18th century Ledbury became, with Hereford, the chief cider market in the county. With the arrival of the Herefordshire and Gloucestershire canal at Ledbury in 1798, many hogsheads of cider found their way both to the traditional markets of Bristol and

62   HAS, 18/4/5, will of Richard Wooding, 1610, 15/1/40, will of William Went, 1667.
63   HAS, AA63/2, p. 92; AA63/3, p. 176; AA63/9, pp. 47, 59.
64   Above, Settlement and Population, Built Environment.
65   HER, 25342, 25344, 25348–9, 25351, 25932–4, 25937–8.
66   HAS, AS94/101.
67   *Hereford Times*, 7 Dec., 14 Dec. 1867.
68   Duncumb, *General View*, 64; John Lodge, *Sketches towards a Topographical History of the County of Hereford* (1793), 33.
69   E.L. Jones, 'Agricultural conditions and changes in Herefordshire, 1660–1815', *TWNFC*, 37 (1961), 35; Valentine Green, *The History and Antiquities of the City and Suburbs of Worcester* II (1796), 18–19.
70   Duncumb, *General View*, 65; *Hereford Times*, 31 Aug., 7 Sept., 7 Dec. 1867.
71   *Kelly's Dir. Herefs.* (1934); HAS, AS94/209, sale cat.
72   British Hop Association: http://www.britishhops.org.uk (accessed 13 Dec. 2015).
73   e.g. HAS, 34/4/52, will of William Powell 1591.
74   HAS, 1/5/8, will of Anthony Huck, 1658; 8/4/23, will of William Brown, 1665.
75   http://www.bosburyhistoryresource.org.uk/Barland-pear (accessed 17 May 2016).
76   HAS, AS94/101.

Figure 9 *Hop pickers on Old Court farm in the 1950s, all of them local people.*

London, and also via the Severn into the industrial Midlands. Barges also carried fresh apples to these markets.[77] Mid 19th-century sales particulars regularly mentioned the 'excellent cider' produced on the property or the 'land well planted with choice fruit trees'.[78] No doubt the opening of the rail connection from Ledbury to Worcester and beyond in 1861 provided better access to the West Midlands for both hops and cider, but also brought hop-pickers from the new conurbation. During the 20th century there was a considerable decline in orcharding, but there has been a revival: in 2015 some farms cropped their orchards under contract to Bulmers and from 2004 until *c.*2014 there was some local cider production.[79]

Farms, Crops and Livestock

In 1801, just over half the area under cultivation, 508 a., was reported to have been sown with wheat, 112 a. with peas, 104 a. with beans, 84 a. with oats, 72 a. with turnips, 31 a. with barley, 12 a. with rye and 10 a. with potatoes. There were a large number of apple and pear trees and significant hop grounds which together reduced the average production of wheat per acre to 12 bushels.[80]

    Between 1851 and 1881 farms recorded by the census enumerators ranged in size from fewer than 10 a. to over 400 a.; the acreage of individual farms varied as farmers

77   Lodge, *Sketches towards a Topographical History*, 96; Jones, 'Agricultural conditions and changes in Herefordshire', 35–6.
78   *Hereford Jnl*, 25 May, 6 July 1867.
79   e.g. Temple Court, http://bosaherefords.co.uk/index.php/sarahs-cider (accessed 13 Dec. 2015); local inf.
80   *Home Office Acreage Returns* (HO67) (List & Index Soc. 189, 1982), 191, 197–8.

gave up or took on land. In 1851, 40 farms were recorded, the largest being William Pitt's 390 a. at Temple Court, closely followed by Thomas Inett's 387 a. at Old Court. Five other farms covered 200 a. or more: The Farm (300 a.), Gold Hill (250 a.), Nashend (218 a.), Upleadon Court (220 a.) and Cold Green (200 a.). Six farms covered between 199 a. and 100 a., while 13 had fewer than 15 a. By 1861 Old Court, then farmed by Richard Hickman, had increased to 410 a., and Gold Hill to 300 a., while The Farm was still 302 a., and Temple Court had declined to 288 a.; Lower House (217 a.), Nash End (214 a.), and Upleadon Court (200 a.) had all increased in size. In 1871 Old Court, at 400 a., was still by far the largest farm, followed by Gold Hill (305 a.) and Temple Court (305 a.); Barland (possibly The Farm which is otherwise unrecorded that year) contained 260 a., 'Swinmore' (probably Upleadon Court since it was farmed by George Shayle) 230 a., and Nashend 217 a. Farm sizes were similar in 1881, except that the farm attached to Bosbury House had increased in size to 210 a.[81] In 1910 Old Court farm (367 a.) was still the largest farm in the parish, followed by The Farm (329 a.); Gold Hill contained only 280 a., Nash End had increased to 261 a., and Temple Court had been reduced to 249 a.[82]

By the early 1940s, 66 farms covered almost the whole parish: 4,623 a. out of 4,827 a.[83] Fourteen of the farms had over 100 a., the largest being Old Court (472 a.), followed by The Farm (336 a.), Nelmes (280 a.), Cold Green (249 a.), and Temple Court (220 a.).[84] The smallest of the 66 farms were the 21 smallholdings of fewer than 15 a., 15 of them apparently cottage farmers, as they employed no staff. Sixteen of the farms grew hops, Old Court (50 a.) and Cold Green (46 a.) having the largest acreages. There were 542 a. of orchards, the highest acreages being at the Nelmes (58 a.), Slatch (48 a.) and Gold Hill (40 a.). Just under 30 per cent of the acreage was under arable cultivation (1,306¼ a.); the chief crops were wheat, oats and mixed corn, but peas, potatoes, beans, mangolds, sugar beet, turnips and swedes, kale, lucerne (alfalfa) and vegetables were also grown. The farms employed 92 full-time, regular workers and 76 casual (seasonal) or part-time workers, the largest numbers being employed on the largest farms, although Cold Green employed slightly more workers than Old Court, presumably because it produced more labour-intensive crops or animals. Grazing, having declined during the 19th century, seems to have been growing in importance: just over half the land (2,774 a.) was grazing land, supporting just over 1,500 cattle and a similar number of sheep, with 120 steers and 139 horses. The highest numbers were at Old Court with 148 cattle and 114 sheep; The Farm had 104 cattle, Brook Inn had 148 sheep, and Gold Hill had 118 sheep. Only six farms had no cattle, but 35 had no sheep.

Mixed farming continued in the later 20th century and the early 21st; hops retained their importance, and new orchards were planted. In 1986 most of the farms were comparatively small at under 100 a. Wheat was the principal grain crop, with hops and fruit, presumably mainly apples; dairy cattle and sheep were kept.[85] Stock farming was severely affected by the foot and mouth epidemic of 1967 but suffered only restrictions on movement in that of 2002. A herd of Hereford cattle was established on Temple

81   TNA, HO 107/197; TNA, RG 9/1809; RG 10/2681; RG 11/2581.
82   TNA, IR 58/38651–3.
83   Paragraph based on TNA, MAF 32/3/147.
84   In both 1924 and 1945 Nelmes was recorded as having 167 a.: HAS, M5/5/32, M5/5/33
85   Domesday project 1986, copy at http://www.bosburyhistoryresource.org.uk/DomesdayProject1986 (accessed 17 May 2016).

Court farm in 1981, and by 2015 comprised 90 cows. In 2012 it won the National Herd of the Year award.[86] By 2016 farms had been amalgamated, and many farmhouses sold as private houses. At Nashend the farm buildings were developed for housing. Apart from the smallholdings on the Buchanan Trust Estate, described below, only nine farms remained: Catley Cross, Cold Green, Grange, Note House, Old Court, Temple Court, The Farm, Townend, and Upleadon. Townend specialised in hops, and had an award-winning holiday cottage.[87]

The Buchanan Trust or Bosbury Farm Settlement

In 1915 Robert Buchanan of Bosbury House approached the Board of Agriculture and Fisheries about giving land for an ex-soldiers' settlement, as a memorial to his son Alan, killed that year. An Act of Parliament was necessary before the Board could accept the gift,[88] and it was not until 1918 that a deed was signed, transferring *c.*288 a. of the Bosbury House estate, including Nashend and neighbouring farms, to the Board.[89] Another *c.*500 a. in the same area were conveyed in July 1919. By the spring of 1921 the estate consisted of 14 holdings, 21 cottages, 102 a. of woodlands, and 2 a. of rough pasture at Beacon Hill. The new cottages, farm buildings, hutments and adaptations were finished and all that remained to be done was to sink three wells.[90]

The work involved heavy capital expenditure by the Ministry of Agriculture: £23,070, almost as much as the total value of the estate in 1922 (£24,500).[91] As well as facing financial problems, the Ministry had difficulty from the outset in finding tenants, who were required to have served overseas.[92] As early as 1926 the Trustees were in correspondence with the Charity Commission about widening the terms of benefit, and in 1932 they were allowed to let land to any ex-servicemen, or failing them any suitable persons in need of assistance.[93]

In 1952, the estate was designated under section 50 of the Agriculture Act 1947 as being held for the purposes of smallholdings. As well as having implications for the selection of tenants, the designation enabled tenants to apply for government loans for working capital, and allowed the estate to receive money voted in Parliament for capital works. Improvements to farm equipment and water supplies took place in the next few years.[94]

Following the 1967 foot and mouth outbreak, when most of the tenants lost their stock, the estate was reorganized.[95] Under a Charity Commission Scheme, Herefordshire County Council was appointed trustee with powers to administer the charity. The

86   http://www.bosaherefords.co.uk (accessed 2 Jan. 2016).
87   http://www.thecornmillhereford.co.uk (accessed 13 May 2016).
88   Sailors and Soldiers (Gifts for Land Settlement) Act Ch. 60 6&7 Geo. 5 [22 Dec. 1916]; *Hereford Times*, 2 Dec. 1916, p.2.
89   TNA, MAF 48/310 [photocopy at HAS, CP85/1/1].
90   TNA, MAF 48/311, MAF 48/312; MAF 174/109, conveyance dated 1 July 1919.
91   *Western Morning News*, 3 Oct. 1922.
92   TNA, MAF 139/82.
93   TNA, MAF 174/109. 24 Apr. 1926; MAF 48/592; Charity Commission Scheme 31 May 1932, http://www.buchanan-trust.co.uk/Charity (accessed 3 Sept. 2015).
94   TNA, MAF 174/109, letters dated 1 and 7 Apr. 1952; minute dated 10 June 1955.
95   TNA, MAF 174/109, Bosbury Trust Estate Report, 1968.

estate then comprised 676 a., let to various tenants for rents amounting to £5307.75.[96] Herefordshire County Council was succeeded by the new Hereford and Worcester Council in 1974, then by Herefordshire Council in 1998. The Trust estate has been managed with the other council smallholdings, though with the involvement of the Buchanan Trust in the selection of suitably qualified ex-servicemen. After lengthy consultations between 2012 and 2014, new trustees took control of the estate (693 a. let in 11 holdings) in November 2015.[97]

Industry and Crafts

Mills

There was a mill on Bosbury manor in 1086.[98] About 1288 it was a watermill held with 9 a. of land and paying the bishop 24*s.* 3*d.* a year, although the annual income from the mill was reported to be less than 16*s.* in silver. By *c.*1308 the mill was farmed for only 20*s.* a year.[99] In 1578, when it was held by Gabriel Halfield, the mill was a water mill called Wyll mill; it stood on the Leadon south of the village.[100] In 1703 the mill, then called Lower Mill, was held with two meadows or pastures called Wyll Mill. In 1722 it was described as a water corn mill, as it was in 1753 when it was called Lower or Will Mill.[101] The house and mill appear to have been rebuilt during the 19th century and the mill was still working in 1911, but in 1913 was occupied by a farmer.[102] By 1958 it was in a ruinous state, the wheel gone and the pond dried.[103]

A windmill on the bishop's manor had been recently repaired in the later 14th century.[104] In 1496 it was 'totally decayed' and paid no rent. In 1578 a house site stood near the way leading to the windmill, near Windmill Hill field.[105]

There was also a mill on Upleadon manor in 1086.[106] In 1322 a carpenter was paid for making wheels for it, perhaps suggesting that it was a double mill. In 1309 it was farmed for at least 36*s.* 8*d.*, and in 1338, by which time it belonged to the Hospitallers, the watermill was worth 40*s.*[107] The mill was part of the Upleadon or Temple Court estate in 1571 and 1671.[108] A millward of Upleadon mill died in 1670, and there was a miller there

---

96   Charity Commission Scheme 8 February 1972: http://www.buchanan-trust.co.uk/Charity (accessed 3 Sept. 2015).
97   Annual rpt to Charity Commission, 2013–14: http://apps.charitycommission.gov.uk/Accounts (accessed 7 Sept. 2015). Hillhouse farm had been sold in 1997 and Nashend farm in 2001: https://www.streetcheck.co.uk (accessed 13 Dec. 2015); inf. from Robert Buchanan, incoming trustee.
98   *Domesday*, 502.
99   HAS, AA59/A/1, pp. 158–9; TNA, E 199/18/4.
100 HAS, AA59/A/2, ff. 7v., 54v.
101 HAS, AA63/6, p. 76; AA63/9, p. 176.
102 TNA, RG 14/15602; *Kelly's Dir. Herefs.* (1913).
103 *Glos. Soc. for Industrial Archaeology, Newsletter* no. 7 Apr. 1966, http://www.gsia.org.uk (accessed 16 Dec. 2015).
104 TNA, SC 6/1138/5, undated fragment of a compotus roll, perhaps 1360–1.
105 HAS, AM33/13; HAS, AA59/A/2, f. 37.
106 *Domesday*, 512.
107 TNA, SC 6/860/19; TNA, E358/18; Larking (ed.), *Knights Hospitallers in England*, 195.
108 TNA, E 150/456/1; TNA, CP 25/2/661.

in 1702 and 1704.[109] In 1726 and 1748 the mill was called Mannings mill, from Francis Mannings (d. 1711), miller there by 1702. By 1810 it was Upper mill, to distinguish it from Lower mill, and between 1851 and 1861 it became Dodds mill.[110] It stood on the Leadon near the Bishop's Frome boundary in the extreme north of the parish. It was still working in 1911, but had ceased by 1913.[111] The timber-framed building, which was converted into a house in the mid 20th century, was probably originally 17th-century, but was refaced in 1788 and further altered in the 20th century.[112]

Extractive industries

In the late 1740s Charles Bennet paid for considerable quantities of stone to be 'raised' or quarried, presumably locally, to repair the barn at Temple Court. In 1847 a load of stone was hauled from Bentley's Quarry to Dowdings brook for the parish surveyor.[113] Two quarries, four Quarry fields and a Quarry meadow occur in the tithe award of 1839, and the Ordnance Survey map of 1885 marked five quarries and three old quarries; they were mainly on the higher ground in the north of the parish but one of the quarry fields was at Swinmore.[114] Most were probably worked intermittently on a small scale, but between 1813 and 1851 at least six masons or stonemasons lived, and may have worked, in the parish.[115] In 1919 stone was quarried on site for roads and foundations of the Farm Settlement.[116] The gravel quarry, shown on the tithe map, and the gravel pit, on that of 1885, probably both supplied material for road-mending.[117]

A Bosbury man bequeathed an iron bolt 'in the brickyard', presumably in Bosbury, in 1544, and in 1616 Philip Stanton wanted his tombstone walled round with brick.[118] A Brick Clamp piece and Kiln Orchard were named in the tithe award of 1839, and two clay pits on the map of 1885.[119] The bankrupt Robert Drew in 1824 had been 'maltster, timber merchant, brickmaker, dealer and chapman'.[120] Most early brickmaking was probably done on site, as needed, but in the mid 19th century there was some commercial brickmaking. In 1851 John Hodges, brickmaker at Pow Green, employed four young lads; in 1861 Hodges was described as a labourer, but his grandson worked at the brickyard with two other young men. That year two brickmakers lived in a hut at the brickyard near Staplow Wharf.[121] There are no later references to brickmaking in the parish.

109 HAS, 27/2/27, will of William Alcocke, 1670; Par. Rec., baptism register.
110 HAS, AA63/10, p. 58; HAS, AA63/12, p. 242; Par. Rec., baptism 1702, burials 1711, 1810; TNA, HO 107/1975; TNA, RG 9/1809.
111 TNA, RG 14/15602; *Kelly's Dir. Herefs.* (1913).
112 NHL, no. 1302714, Dodds Mill (accessed 31 Jul. 2015).
113 HAS, AS94/101, pp. 24, 26; HAS, BS78.
114 HER, 18263, 18271, 18277, 18278, 18280, 18327, 40077, 40080, 40128-9, 40131-3, 40409.
115 Par. Rec., baptisms 1813, 1816, 1819, 1824, 1827, 1829-31, 1838-43, 1845, 1847, 1849-51.
116 TNA, CAB 24/92.
117 HER, 18277, 41283.
118 HAS, 32/1/1, will of Nicholas ap Powell 1544; TNA, PROB 11/128 will of Philip Stanton, 1616.
119 HER, 18256, 32412, 41247, 41291.
120 *London Gaz.*, 23 Mar. 1824.
121 TNA, HO 107/197; TNA, RG 9/1809.

Figure 10 *The chairmaker Philip Clissett (d. 1913) in his workshop, surrounded by his tools.*

Crafts

Most of the residents of Bosbury before the mid 20th century were engaged in agriculture to varying degrees. Even those described as craftsmen also farmed on a small to middling scale, like the tailor William Cowles (d. 1681), who owned a cow, two pigs, hay and a cider mill, or the cordwainer Robert Meadowcourt (d. 1667) who owned cows, oxen, a sheep and pigs as well as grain, hay, cheese and cider.[122] This combining of occupations continued through the 19th century, as in the case of Robert Drew, mentioned above. The main alternative to agricultural work was domestic service. The 1841 census recorded 153 agricultural labourers, 23 general labourers, 73 domestic servants and 4 gardeners, a total of 253. By 1911 the number working in these sectors had reduced to 186, of whom 142 worked in agricultural and 42 in domestic occupations; the remaining two were general labourers.[123]

Carpenters and other woodworkers, like John Mutlow who in 1604 passed his coopery tools to his sons,[124] occur frequently between the 17th and the 19th centuries. Some of them, like the glazier whose children were baptised in 1627 and 1629,[125] probably worked in the building trade. In the 19th century their numbers declined

122 HAS, 70/2/32, will of William Cowles, 1681; 16/1/22 will of Robert Meadowcourt, 1667.
123 TNA, HO 107/424/5; TNA, RG 14/15602.
124 HAS, 7/1/30 will of John Mutlow, 1604.
125 Par. Rec., baptism register.

from 15 in 1841 to two in 1911.[126] A joiner was 'late of Bosbury' in 1712, and four wheelwrights, and a lath cleaver were recorded in the baptismal registers between 1813 and 1851.[127]

The best-known Bosbury woodworker was Philip Clissett (1817–1913), a member of a chairmaking family living at Birtsmorton (Worcs.). After his marriage to a Bosbury girl, Philip set up his home and workshop at Stanley Hill near the small New Hill wood in Bosbury and coppice woods in Castle Frome; he was later assisted there by his sons and other members of his family. Clissett sold his chairs in Hereford and other local markets until a visit to his workshop in 1886 by the architect James MacLaren, influential in the Arts and Crafts movement. Collaboration between the two men enhanced Clissett's reputation as a designer and craftsman.[128] His work was further popularised by the success of the workshop of Ernest Gimson and Edward Gardiner who were influenced by his designs and methods.[129] Examples of Clissett's work are now in the Victoria and Albert Museum as well as in local collections.

Blacksmiths were first recorded in the parish in 1578, when a smith lived at the Black House.[130] A William Palmer was recorded as a blacksmith in 1764, and another blacksmith of the same name in 1823 owned a blacksmith's shop, hopyard and orchard again indicating multiple occupations.[131] In the mid and later 19th century there were blacksmiths' or shoeing smiths' shops in the village itself, at Pow Green to the east and at Stanley Hill to the north west, ensuring easy access from all the farms to this vital service. In 1891 the innkeeper at the Oak at Staplow was also a blacksmith, and in 1901 a blacksmith occupied Staplow Wharf.[132]

Among the 17th-century cloth- and clothing workers recorded in the parish were several tailors at different dates,[133] clothworkers in 1614, 1631 and 1702,[134] five weavers between 1612 and 1645 and one in 1717,[135] and a fuller in 1590.[136] Spinners were recorded in 1619 and 1623, four breeches makers between 1775 and 1780, and a flax dresser in 1701.[137] In 1851 and 1861 a handful of elderly widows worked at spinning and carding, activities which in earlier centuries would have occupied much of the time of the women of the parish. Many cordwainers and shoemakers were recorded in the 17th and 18th

---

126 TNA, HO 107/424/5; TNA, RG 14/15602.

127 Par. Rec. baptism register; HAS, AR67/72.

128 For Clissett see F.C. Morgan, 'Philip Clissett, a Bosbury chair-maker', *TWNFC*, 32 (1946), 16–18; *Hereford Times*, 1 Feb. 1913, *Hereford Jnl*, 1 Feb. 1913; http://www.philipclissett.co.uk (accessed 30 Mar. 2016).

129 Bernard D. Cotton, *The English Regional Chair* (London, 1990).

130 HAS, 45/4/76 will of William Woodyatt 1597; HAS, 27/3/19 will of James Alcock 1614; HAS, 54/1/9 will of William Parsons, 1677; HAS, AA59/2 f. 29; Par. Rec., baptism register.

131 Par. Rec., baptism register; HAS, HD5/1, no. 132210

132 TNA, HO 107/1975; RG 9/1809; RG 10/2681; TNA, RG 10/2681; TNA, RG 13/2470.

133 HAS, 7/6/32 will Thomas Knight, 1605; HAS, 5/3/26 will of Richard Knight, 1664; HAS, 70/2/32 will of William Cowles. 1681.

134 HAS, 63A/1/53 will of Henry Mutlow, 1614; 41/1/2 will of Paul Stephens, 1631; Par. Rec. baptism register.

135 HAS, 16/3/48 will of John Hall, 1612; 39/1/61 will of Richard Dalley, 1628; 44/1/6, will of Richard Woodyatt, 1633; 56/4/8 will of Thomas Holman, 1645; Par. Rec., baptism register 1717.

136 TNA, PROB 11/77, will of Thomas Lawrence, 1590.

137 HAS, 20/3/20, will of Elizabeth Alcock, 1619; 33/1/73, will of Thomas Alcock, 1623; Par. Rec., baptism register.

centuries.[138] By 1841 tailors, shoemakers and a dressmaker were working in the main street.[139] A milliner and two glovers were also recorded in the late 17th and the early 18th century, perhaps working for Ledbury masters.[140] Bosbury's proximity to Worcester provided opportunities in the putting-out glove industry and by 1851 as many as 40 women were working in the trade. As glove-making became more mechanized and work moved into factories, the number of Bosbury gloveresses declined, to *c.*20 between 1861 and 1881 and to only four a decade later.[141]

Professional Occupations

In addition to the vicars, and the schoolmasters, resident for much of Bosbury's history, doctors were recorded in the mid 20th century. In 1929 Leslie Drake MB, CM was listed in the parish, as was Alfred Gollard, resident physician at Holly Mount, which was being run as a rest home for nurses. William Webster, a physician, was resident in the village in 1941, as was Beatrice Hill, district nurse. At other times Bosbury residents went to

Figure 11 *The recently opened General Stores in Main Street c.1905.*

---

138 Par. Rec., baptism register; HAS, 26/4/25, will of John Knight, 1567; 16/1/22, will of Robert Meadowcourt, 1667.

139 TNA, HO 107/424/5.

140 HAS, 97/1/8 will of Thomas Chadd 1687; 110/4/1 will of John Smith 1691; Par. Rec., baptisms 1703; S. Pinches, *Ledbury: a market town and its Tudor heritage* (Chichester, 2009), 35–9.

141 TNA, HO 107/1975; TNA, RG 9/1809; RG 11/2581; RG 12/2051; Pinches, *Ledbury*, 99–102.

doctors in Ledbury or Cradley.[142] Ledbury, the nearest market town, also provides and has provided other professional services.

Commerce

Butchers, who presumably sold meat in the village, were recorded in 1603, 1751 and 1764, and a baker in 1702 and 1704.[143] Shops, which may have been workshops as well as places for selling goods, were recorded in the main street in 1708 and 1718, and there was a shopkeeper there in 1769.[144]

In 1851, there was a grocer and tea dealer and two butchers, one of whom was also a shopkeeper, and a shop at the Bell inn. In 1863, however, only two grocers were listed in directories, and in 1871 only one grocer, two butchers and a shopkeeper appeared in the census returns. By 1885 there were a butcher, a grocer, three shopkeepers (one also a farmer), and a coal merchant in the parish. In 1891 there were grocer's and butcher's shops in the village, with another butcher at The Nest; the only other commercial enterprise was the coal and timber merchant who was still based at Staplow Wharf although the canal had long closed.[145] The General Stores in the main street was opened *c*.1905 by Uriah Cosford who had formerly run a draper's shop in Worcester. In 1934 it advertised groceries, drapery and provisions, and by 1937 it had expanded into petrol and oils for motorists as well as becoming a newsagents and tobacconists. In 1941, perhaps because of rationing restrictions during the war, it was only a grocers.[146]

In addition to the Stores, the 1941 directory listed two blacksmiths, an agricultural implement repairers and a water diviner in the parish.[147] The general stores, a butcher and garage all advertised their services into the 1970s; the general stores closed *c*.2000, but a bakery survived until 2002 or later. Eventually no Bosbury shop was able to compete with supermarkets and a range of other shops in Ledbury. The Bosbury Press, a small printing firm, was based in the village in the 1970s and early 1980s. By the late 20th century a number of villagers were running small businesses from domestic premises, including garden design and piano restoration.[148] By 2015 there were two service providers: Stanley House Care Home specialising in patients with Huntington's disease, and Jack-in-the-Box Nursery for children in the village.[149] An agricultural plastics recycling business was based at North Farm, and a blacksmith's forge specialising in ornamental wrought iron at Hillhouse farm.[150]

---

142 *Kelly's Dir Herefs.* (1929, 1941); local inf.
143 HAS, A81/11/5; HAS, AA63/15 p.154; Par. Rec., baptism register, 1702, 1704.
144 HAS, AA63/6, p. 272; AA63/9, p. 32; AA63/16, p. 65.
145 TNA, RG 10/2681; RG 12/2015; *Lascelles Dir. Herefs.* (1851); *P.O. Dir. Herefs.* (1863); *Kelly's Dir. Herefs.* (1885); for the canal see above, Introduction (Communications).
146 TNA, RG 14/15602; *Grantham Jnl*, 2 May 1931, obituary of Uriah Cosford, http://www. bosburyhistoryresource.org.uk, (accessed 1 Jan. 2016); *Kelly's Dir. Herefs.* (1934, 1937, 1941).
147 *Kelly's Dir. Herefs.* (1926, 1941).
148 *Tilley's Ledbury Almanack*, 1966, 1970, 1973, 1976, 1979, 2000, 2002; *Ledbury Reporter*, 26 Aug. 1980: http://www.bosburyhistoryresource.org.uk (accessed 16 May 2016).
149 http://www.stanleyhousecare.co.uk, http://www.jackintheboxnursery.co.uk (accessed 9 Nov. 2015).
150 http://www.farmplasticsrecycled.co.uk and http://www.oliverdakersblacksmith.co.uk (accessed 13 Dec. 2015).

SOCIAL HISTORY

Social Structure

13th to 18th Centuries

ON THE BISHOP'S BOSBURY MANOR in the 1280s there were, in addition to the three men who held by knight service, eleven freeholders. Their holdings ranged from 1½ yardlands to a messuage and curtilage (probably a house, outbuildings, garden and yard). An additional 13 tenants held freely small amounts of forlet land, and one held a few acres of demesne land. A total of 27 tenants held customary land, 17 of them yardlands. The status of the 25 tenants who owed the bishop a 'gift' at the feast of St Andrew (30 November), often with honey or fish at the Annunciation (25 March), is unclear; some were certainly customary tenants, but others may have been small freeholders. On the sub-manor held by the rector of the church, there were 12 freeholders, and three unfree tenants.[1] Although the numbers of free and customary tenants were nearly equal, in terms of the size of their holdings the customary tenants would have dominated the manor.

The medieval bishops, particularly Bishops Cantilupe and Swinfield, visited Bosbury regularly as they toured their manors with their household.[2] Bishop Swinfield's accounts for 1289–90 record that produce from Bosbury, including grain and venison, was regularly sent to other manors. The bishop's main store of wine was kept there, and large quantities of ale were brewed. When he stayed in the manor Bishop Swinfield seems mainly to have consumed the produce of the demesne, although the salmon, eels and cod he ate in June 1290 must have been purchased or brought from elsewhere. Later that year a cart was sent from Bosbury to London to collect cloth, furs and spices ordered for the bishop.[3] Litigants and others came to see the bishop, as in 1286 when, in Bosbury church, he arbitrated in a dispute between the abbot of Lyre (Eure, Normandy) and the Hereford dean and chapter. At least one house on the manor was later held by an official of the bishop's household: in 1355 Bishop Trilleck leased to John le Chamberlain, his wife and son, a tenement which had been held by William the beadle.[4]

There were several freeholders on Upleadon manor, like Richard Ruyhale who died early in 1408 holding a small estate in Catley, Upleadon and Bosbury of the Hospitallers. Joan and Alice Pouke of Catley, who dealt with land in Ledbury in 1328, were probably

1   HAS, AA59/A1, pp. 153–9.
2   See the published bishops' registers, particularly *Reg. Cantilupe* and *Reg. Swinfield*, passim.
3   *Roll of the Household Expenses of Richard de Swinfield bishop of Hereford during part of the years 1289 and 1290*, ed. John Webb (Camden Soc., 1855), passim.
4   *Reg. Swinfield*, 117; HCA, 2454.

of some standing.[5] Eleven people held freehold land in 1505, some only a few acres, others a yardland or more.[6] Humphrey son of William Lyne who held two yardlands called Marriets was succeeded by his son John Lyne of Paunceford Court, Munsley, who held the estate at his death in 1559.[7] The Nelmes comprised a freehold yardland held in 1505 by William Watts; by 1590 it had passed to William Lawrence through Anne wife of Peter Lawrence.[8] Another freehold yardland called Cachfrench had by 1505 been divided into two half yardlands, one held by Simon Melbourne esquire of Tillington Court in Burghill. It was probably one of those half yardlands which John Dobbins held at his death in 1553.[9]

For the subsidy of 1524, a total of 18 people were assessed in Upleadon: one, Thomas Myntriche, on land, 14 on goods, and three on wages.[10] Thomas's father James Myntriche (d. 1512 or 1513) was in Bosbury by 1488 when he was executor of another parishioner's will.[11] The family's estate may have been that later called Catley manor.[12] The highest assessment on goods was Humphrey Farley's £10, followed by Roger Alcott's £6 13s. 4d. In 1505 Humphrey Farley held a half yardland, and later acquired a further three half yardlands; in 1528 he, or another man of the same name, held three copyholds of Upleadon manor. In 1569 a Humphrey Farley registered a coat of arms at the herald's visitation.[13]

At Bosbury, 24 people were assessed, none on land, 22 on goods and two on wages.[14] Edward Walwyn, John Halfhide (or Hawfield), and Richard Hope were assessed on £20 worth of goods each, double the highest Upleadon assessment and three times the next highest Bosbury assessment of £6 13s. 4d. John Halfhide held the freehold estate of the Grange. Richard Hope, a member of a family established in Bosbury since the 1430s, may have been the same man who held a half yardland in Upleadon in 1505; he may already have been living at Raceys in Bosbury, which John Hope held in 1577, although neither was assessed in 1545. In the 1520s Richard, or another man of the same name with a house in Bosbury, was under-bailiff of Salisbury (Wiltshire).[15] Edward Walwyn, who lived in Coddington, was a member of the knightly family who held extensive lands in south-east Herefordshire.[16]

5   *Cal. Inq. p.m.* XIX, no. 400, p. 140; cf. TNA, CP 25/1/83/51, no. 17: http://www.medievalgenealogy.org.uk/fines/abstracts, (accessed 10 Apr. 2013); HCA, 3274–5.
6   HAS, A63/III/23/1, ff. 7v.–10v.
7   TNA, E 150/450/5; TNA, SC 2/176/102, court 23 Sept. 4 Edw. VI.
8   TNA, LR 3/21/3, court 11 May 32 Eliz. I; TNA, SC 2/176/102, court 11 Apr. 2 Edw. VI.
9   Robinson, *Mansions and Manors*, 54, 117; TNA, SC 2/176/102, court 13 Apr. 7 Edw. VI.
10   M.A. Faraday (ed.) *Herefs. Taxes in the Reign of Henry VIII*, 68.
11   M.A. Faraday (ed.) *Cal. Probate and Administration Acts 1407–1550 in the Consistory Court of Hereford* (Logaston, 2008), 125, 194.
12   Myntriche land in Stoke Lacy passed to the Berringtons in the 16th century: Robinson, *Mansions and Manors*, 260; above, Land Ownership.
13   HAS, A63/II/23/1, f. 8; TNA, C 1/918/49–50; F.W. Weaver (ed.), *The Visitation of Herefordshire made by Robert Cooke, Clarencieux, in 1569* (Exeter, 1886), 87.
14   Faraday (ed.) *Herefs. Taxes in the Reign of Henry VIII*, 70.
15   HAS, A63/II/23/1, f. 7v.; TNA, C 1/540/42; M.A. Faraday (ed.), *Cal. of Probate and Administration Acts 1407–1550 in the Court Bks of the Bishop of Hereford*, 14, 257.
16   Robinson, *Mansions and Manors*, 70, 198–203.

All 64 people assessed for subsidy in the parish in 1545 were assessed on goods. The highest valuation was the £10 on which Richard Lawrence and John Watkins the younger were assessed, but they were not outstandingly wealthy: five people were assessed on £9 worth of goods, six on £8, three on £7, three on £6, three on £5.[17]

In the 1530s Richard Knight, a Bosbury smith, was related to one of the bailiffs of Worcester. In the 1550s John Aburforth of Bosbury, perhaps of Upleadon as the name is not recorded on Bosbury manor, claimed land and goods in Thaxted (Essex) inherited from both his parents. In 1607 James Leeth of Seal (Kent) claimed a copyhold estate in Bosbury which had belonged to his father. In 1656 George Farley of St Giles Cripplegate, London, claimed two houses in Bosbury village.[18]

A survey of the bishop's Bosbury manor in 1578 recorded 10 freeholders holding 12 messuages, six of them 'unbuilt', i.e. demolished or fallen down; customary tenants, including several gentlemen, held 17 messuages, nine of them 'unbuilt'. Six tenants, three of whom held copyholds, were described as gentlemen: James Halfhide or Hawfield of the Grange, John Hope of Raceys, John Scudamore of Temple Court, John Myntridge or Myntriche of the Upleadon family (above), Richard Morton, and Robert Gower.[19] Richard Morton was the son of Rowland Morton, formerly of the Grange.[20] Robert Gower has not been identified. In addition to these six men, Martha Harford, who held a small customary estate, was the widow of Richard Harford, lessee of the bishop's manor and owner of the house later called the Crown.[21]

By 1663 there were greater disparities in wealth in both Bosbury and Upleadon. In both places the highest assessment for maintenance of the militia was £100, more than double the next highest assessment of £40.[22] In Bosbury the £100 was assessed on Thomas Danett; in Upleadon, on the non-resident Sir Robert Pye of Temple Court and on William Brydges, esquire. Danett (d. 1677) was the father of John Danett (d. 1679) whose widow Elizabeth, formerly Brydges, married Bridstock Harford, great grandson of Richard and Martha Harford. John leased Old Court from the Harford family, who by that date were resident in Hereford.[23] William Brydges was brother of Elizabeth; both came from the Old Colwall branch of the family, not that of the related Brydges of Tibberton who built up an estate in Upleadon.[24]

Like the Harfords, several of the wealthier Bosbury families moved away from the parish. In 1676 Giles Powell, who died in Bosbury in 1687, and his wife Anne conveyed a messuage at Nashend to their son, James Powell of London, gentleman.[25] Elizabeth or Betty Powell, widow of Thomas Powell of Bristol, barber surgeon, sold the house in 1719. In 1707 Richard Brydges, citizen and mercer of London, perhaps the son of the William Brydges who was assessed in Bosbury in 1663, surrendered a copyhold croft on Bosbury

17   Faraday (ed.), *Herefs. Taxes in the Reign of Henry VIII*, 309.
18   TNA, C 1/787/26, 27; C 1/1399/2; C 1/1400/1–4; C 3/280/30; C 6/144/61.
19   HAS, AA59/A2, ff. 21v.–54v.
20   Weaver (ed.), *Visitation of Herefs. 1569*, 52; above, Land Ownership.
21   Bentley, *Hist. Bosbury* (1891), 40; F.T. Havergal, *Monumental Inscriptions in the Cathedral Church of Hereford* (London, 1881), 38; above, Settlement and Population (Domestic Architecture).
22   Faraday (ed.), *Herefs. Militia Assessments of 1663*, 92, 102.
23   HAS, 58/1/5, will of Thomas Danett 1678; HAS, 63/1/5, will of John Danett 1679.
24   *Burke's Landed Gentry* (1838 edn), IV. 552.
25   HAS, AA63/3, p. 64; Par. Rec., burial register 1687.

manor. In 1712 Hugh Hughes of the city of London, a worker in gold leaf, was heir to his brother William Hughes of Bosbury, yeoman. On the other hand, Francis Romney, gentleman, who owned Hill house in Nashend, from 1710 or earlier until his death in 1728, lived in the parish and took an active part in some of its affairs, receiving the surrender of a copyhold house in 1725.[26]

Having made a fortune in the United States and Canada, John Stedman, a member of a family recorded in Bosbury since the 16th century, returned to the parish c.1786 and established himself as a country gentleman at Raceys (later Bosbury House). He and James Hartland, the occupier of Temple Court, were the only two Bosbury residents to take game licences in 1788; he served as High Sheriff of Herefordshire in 1798. His will, dated 1786, shows that he owned land in Gloucestershire and Worcestershire as well as Herefordshire.[27]

In the late 1780s the chief landowners in both Bosbury and Upleadon were members of the Brydges family, including Richard Brydges who leased the great tithe from the bishop, Mary Brydges who leased Old Court, and Francis William Thomas Brydges who held Upleadon Court; none of them appears to have lived in the parish.[28] Apart from the Brydges, only one man, James Hartland of Temple Court,[29] held land in both divisions of the parish. In Upleadon just over half the 38 people assessed for land tax in 1786 were assessed on lands worth less than £1. The highest assessment was £14 12s. assessed on the non-resident William Turton of Temple Court; the next highest, a total of £11 12s., on John Mutlow of Cold Green. The remaining landholdings were valued at between £1 and £4. At Bosbury half the 44 people assessed in 1789 held land worth less than £1. The highest assessment after those of Mary Brydges (c.£15) and John Stedman (£13 16s.) was the £6 assessed on Richard Hardwick's estate at The Grange.

19th and 20th Centuries

Marked social disparities continued during the 19th century, the hardship of the poorer parishioners resulting in crimes like sheep stealing, theft of fence rails, and poaching.[30] Emigration contributed to the decline in population from the middle of the century, probably influenced by both economic and religious considerations. In 1861 parish officers paid £20 to assist one family to emigrate to America.[31] At the other extreme of society, five men including Philip Stedman of Raceys, held game licences in 1818.[32]

By the 1840s Bosbury was attracting a new class of gentleman farmers at estates like Temple Court and The Grange.[33] Chief among the newly arrived gentry was the wealthy

26   HAS, AA63/6, p. 247, AA63/7, pp. 65, 212; AA63/9, p. 47, AA63/10, p. 16; Par. Rec., burial register 1728.
27   *Pugh's Hereford Jnl*, 11 Sept. 1788; TNA, PROB 11/1505, both http://www.bosburyhistoryresource.org. uk (accessed 13 Dec. 2015).
28   Except where otherwise noted the following paragraph is based on HAS, Q/REL/6/2–3. For the Brydges family see *Burke's Landed Gentry* (1838 edn) IV, 552.
29   Bentley, *Hist. Bosbury* (1891), 70.
30   *Hereford Jnl*, 25 Mar. 1812, 8 Jun. 1814, 10 Dec. 1817.
31   Emigration records, http://www.bosburyhistoryresource.org.uk (accessed 13 Dec. 2015); Par. Rec., vestry mins, vol. 4, Apr. 1861.
32   *Hereford Jnl*, 23 Sept. 1818.
33   *Hereford Jnl*, 25 Aug. 1841; 14 Apr. 1847.

Figure 12 *The North Ledbury hounds outside the main entrance to Bosbury House, 1910.*

clergyman Edward Higgins (1808–84), a member of an Eastnor family, who acquired
Bosbury House *c.*1828. Higgins became a Justice of the Peace and Deputy Lieutenant
of Herefordshire and Worcestershire, and was a notable antiquarian.[34] He had little
sympathy for the common labourer, pursuing a Cradley labourer in the courts for
digging up two dozen briar stocks in Beacon Hill wood. When 200 labourers gathered at
Bosbury in May 1872 to discuss the formation of a union, Higgins went to the meeting
and accused the outside speaker of spreading falsehoods and making a breach between
labourer and employer. He blamed the labourers' condition on 'the beer shop and early
marriage'.[35] On the other hand, he took an active part in the life of the parish, chairing a
New Year's dinner at the Crown Inn in 1850, and joining the rector in providing a tea to
celebrate the royal wedding in 1863.[36] Higgins's grandson, W.B. Mynors, succeeded him
in his position in the parish.[37]

    Although several farmers employed one general domestic servant, there were few large
households in the parish in 1861, the largest being Edward Higgins's with two housemaids,
a cook, nurse, undernurse, and a 14-year-old page. The vicar L.S.B. Stanhope had a cook,
housemaid, nursemaid and a general servant, and Richard Hickman at Old Court a groom,
housemaid, cook, nurse and nursemaid. By 1891 the number of households with one or
two servants had increased. W.B. Mynors at Bosbury House then employed a butler, a
lady's maid, two housemaids, a page, a cook, a kitchenmaid, and a coachman; at Stanley
House there was a cook, parlourmaid, nurse and groom; the vicar, however, had only two

34   Robinson, *Mansions and Manors*, 35, 109–11; J. Cooper, *Eastnor* (2013), 23, 48–9, 59–60, 74–75; *P.O. Dir. Herefs.* (1863); P. Weaver, *Dict. of Herefs Biog.* (Logaston, 2015), 211.

35   *Hereford Jnl*, 10 Sept., 24 Sept. 1845; *Hereford Times* 7 Dec. 1867; *Berrow's Worcester Jnl*, 4 May 1872.

36   *Hereford Jnl*, 9 Jan. 1850; 14 March 1863: http://www.bosburyhistoryresource.org.uk (accessed 17 Dec. 2015).

37   Above, Land Ownership.

Figure 13 *Portrait of
Mrs Marian Buck, later
of Noverings.*

domestic servants. In 1911 the size of the Mynors' household had been slightly reduced,
but Samuel Willcox at The Grange had a housekeeper, cook, housemaid, under housemaid,
coachman and groom, and at the Noverings the absent Mrs Marian Buck had left a
parlourmaid and a housemaid in charge of her house.[38]

Marian Buck, who had Noverings House built in 1907, played an important part
in the life of the parish when she moved there after retiring from her work developing
cookery training for girls in Leicester and at Evendine Court, Colwall.[39] In 1916 she
gave land on which to build a war memorial.[40] In 1919 she gave land to extend the
churchyard; in 1945 she donated the Parish Rooms (the former vicarage house) to the
community. In 1957 a stained glass window was installed in the church in recognition of
her philanthropic work.[41]

38   TNA, RG 9/1809; RG 12/2051; RG 14/15602.
39   J. Butchart, *Ninety Years On: A History of Evendine Court* (1986), http://www.bosburyhistoryresource.
     org.uk, accessed 13 Dec. 2015.
40   Deed of conveyance 7 June 1916, held at Masefield's Solicitors, Ledbury, inf. from Barry Sharples;
     Hereford Jnl 29 April 1916.
41   Par. Rec., vestry min., vol. 3, 23 April 1919; Par. Rec., parochial church council min., 16 Dec. 1957;
     http://www.bosburyhistoryresource.org.uk, s.v. Marian Buck, accessed 13 Dec. 2015.

Social Life and Recreation

In 1588 James Hill of Bosbury was presented in the ecclesiastical court for having 'unlawful games' in his house during church services.[42] The following year, on the Sunday before Lent, several men refused to attend the evening service, instead playing a form of blind man's buff; one of them when asked for his name replied Robin Hood. This was presumably some sort of traditional Shrovetide game. The same year an ale-house keeper was accused of being a 'common dancer on the sabbath'.[43]

More respectable entertainments were recorded in the 19th century. In January 1844 a ploughing match took place at The Farm, followed by refreshments at the Crown. In 1867 the landlord of the Bell organised pigeon shoots followed by dinner. In 1869 a fundraising event for the Boys Grammar School, held at Old Court, included the singing of 'glees and choruses', and in the same year the vicar J.E. Cheese caused much mirth with an evening class of 'Penny Readings'.[44]

The Bosbury Friendly Society met at the Crown inn in the later 18th century, and an Amicable Society, established in 1794 met at the Bell inn.[45] J.H. Underwood, vicar from 1830 to 1856, was among those who encouraged the establishment of a branch of the Swinfield Lodge of Oddfellows. The Oddfellows Lodge in the village opened with a public dinner at the Crown in 1869.[46] The Swinfield Lodge of Oddfellows held regular meetings at the same inn in 1875.[47]

An agricultural show, founded in 1847 for Bosbury, Colwall, Coddington, Wellington Heath, Mathon, Cradley and Storridge, was held in Bosbury from the 1870s until 1969.[48] The format varied but at times included horse racing, classes for showing horses, cattle, sheep, vegetables, fruit, flowers and other local produce, including eggs, honey, cakes and preserves. In 1867 several cottagers from Bosbury won prizes of between 2s. 6d. and 10s. for the most productive gardens.[49] Special categories included vine training and hand-made garden tools.

By the early 20th century there were active cricket teams for men and women with regular matches held between the two.[50] The club closed sometime before the Second World War, but was active again between 1945 and 1969. It restarted in 1981 and in 2015 played in a local league. In 1986 a youth club met in premises behind the parish hall; activities included badminton and table tennis.

42   HAS, HD4/1/153, f. 138v.
43   HAS, HD4/1/155, courts 15 Apr., 29 July 1589; D.N. Klausner (ed.), *Recs. of Early English Drama: Herefordshire and Worcestershire* (Toronto, 1990), 66, 274.
44   *Hereford Jnl,* 3 Jan. 1844, 19 March 1845, 2 Feb. 1867, 17 Apr. 1869; *Berrow's Worcester Jnl*, 20 Nov. 1869.
45   F.C. Morgan, 'Friendly Societies in Herefordshire', *TWNFC* (1946), 183–211.
46   *Kington Reporter,* 22 Aug. 1914 (death and funeral of W.B. Mynors); *Hereford Jnl,* 3 Apr. 1869.
47   Morgan, 'Friendly Societies in Herefordshire', 183–211; *Littlebury's Dir. Herefs,* (1876).
48   Unless otherwise stated, paragraph based on http://www.bosburyhistoryresource.org.uk (accessed 13 Dec. 2015).
49   *Hereford Jnl*, 20 July 1867.
50   Paragraph based on material on http://www.bosburyhistoryresource.org.uk (accessed 13 Dec. 2015).

Figure 14 *Horses and riders at the Bosbury Show, 1907; a marquee can be seen in the background.*

Figure 15 *Ladies' and gentlemen's cricket teams after a match, 1909.*

Parish Hall

In 1911 the old vicarage was converted into parish rooms. In 1945 Marian Buck donated the building to a charitable trust with trustees representing organisations using the rooms, including the British Legion, Women's Institute, the Men's Club, Youth Club, Garden Club, Tennis Club, Mothers' Union, Home Guard and the Girl Guides as well as the managers of the boys' and girls' schools.[51] A new parish hall was built in 1968. A sports hall was added in the 1970s and retail premises in 1998. A tennis court and bowling green opened in 1996. In 2007 further improvements were made, including a new entrance.[52] The hall is owned and maintained by Bosbury Parish Hall, a registered charity.[53] In 2015 clubs and activities run there included the Women's Institute, Beavers and Cubs, Bosbury Players, Bosbury Chroniclers, a pilates class, regular farmers' markets and film-showings.[54] Bosbury Barbers traded from the retail premises.

Inns

In the early 1620s and in 1670 there were three ale-houses on Bosbury manor.[55] Between 1818 and 1828 two ale houses were licensed in the parish each year; from the names of their owners it is clear that they were the Bell and the Crown. All was not always well regulated: in 1835 the vestry instructed the churchwardens to work with the constable to prosecute those disturbing the peace by 'tippling, rioting or gaming'.[56]

The Bell, in the main street, opposite the churchyard, may have been the Blue Bells in 1793, but was certainly the Bell the following year.[57] Sale details for the property in 1812 included stabling for eight horses, malt-house, malt kiln, brew-house and cellar. In 1851 the landlord ran a shop and post office from the premises. In 1910 it and the Crown were both owned by Lane Bros. and Baston of the Vine Brewery, Ledbury.[58] It remained open in 2015.

The Crown inn was built as a private house by the Harfords in the mid 16th century.[59] Sale particulars in 1845 noted the inn had been trading for 35 years, and it was certainly an inn by 1812 when the vestry met there to escape the cold in the church.[60] Between 1917 and 1941 it was known as 'Ye Olde Crown Hotel'.[61] By 1952 it had closed and been converted to a private dwelling.[62]

51   http://www.bosburyparishhall.org.uk (accessed 13 Dec. 2015).
52   Par. Rec., vestry min., May 1955; Par. Rec., parochial church council min., 1995; http://www. bosburyparishhall.org.uk (accessed 9 Nov. 2015); local inf.
53   http://www.charitycommission.gov.uk (accessed 13 Dec. 2015).
54   http://www.bosburyparishhall.org.uk (accessed 9 Nov. 2015).
55   HAS, AM/33, court of 30 March 17 Jas. I; 18 Oct. 20 Jas. I; HAS, AA63/2, p. 70.
56   HAS, Q/CE1, pp. 7–89, *passim.*; Par. Rec., vestry min., vol. 2, May 1835.
57   *Hereford Jnl*, 9 Oct. 1793; F.C. Morgan, 'Friendly Societies in Herefordshire', *TWNFC* (1946), 183–211.
58   J. Eisel and R. Shoesmith, *The Pubs of Bromyard and East Herefordshire* (2003), 157, citing *Hereford Jnl*, 13 Apr. 1812; *Lascelles Dir. Herefs.* (1851); HAS, AG9/48.
59   Above, Settlement and Population.
60   *Hereford Jnl*, 25 Dec., 1844; Par. Rec., vestry min., vol. 1, f. 20.
61   *Kelly's Dir. Herefs.* (1917, 1941).
62   http://www.britishlistedbuildings.co.uk/England/Herefordshire/Bosbury/The Old Crown (accessed 29 Mar. 2016). English Heritage 18 November 1952.

Figure 16 *The Oak inn at Staplow, 2015.*

Other pubs and beer houses opened in the 19th century. In 1881 John Shaw, who had been a beer retailer in the village since 1856, was publican at the New Inn, which had recently been built on the site of an earlier inn, the Bells, burnt down in 1870.[63] The inn was sold in 1887, and in 1910 was owned by Salt & Co. brewers of Burton.[64] It was licensed until 1921, but was sold the following year and converted into two houses.[65] The farmer Charles Hodges was innkeeper at the Brook in 1881, and his successor, James Matthews, another farmer, was selling beer at Dowdings Brook in 1890.[66] In 1910 the Brook was owned by the Royal Wells Brewery of Malvern; it continued as a licensed house until 1941 or later.[67] Kenelm Orgee, beer retailer, was trading at Dallows in 1851. The family ran The Old Country Inn there until the 1890s, as well as farming and keeping a shop.[68] They still owned the premises in 1910 although the inn was run by a lessee. The Old Country remained open until the 1970s.[69] There was another beer-seller at a farm at New Inn between 1881 and 1911.[70]

63   *P.O. Dir. Herefs.* (1856); TNA, RG 11/2581; *Worcestershire Chronicle*, 22 June 1870, http://www. bosburyhistoryresource.org.uk (accessed 15 Dec. 2015).
64   HAS, AS94/213 (sale cat); HAS, AG9/48.
65   *Tilley's Ledbury Almanack* (1921); inf. from Peter Young, Nov. 2015.
66   TNA, RG 11/2581, RG 12/2051; *Jakeman & Carver Dir. Herefs.* (1890).
67   HAS, AG9/48; *Kelly's Dir. Herefs.* (1917, 1941).
68   *Lascelles Dir. Herefs.* (1858); TNA, HO 107/1975; TNA, RG 9/1809; RG 10/2681; RG 11/2581; RG12/2051; *Littlebury's Dir. Herefs.* (1867); *Worcestershire Chronicle*, 26 March 1892, http://www. bosburyhistoryresource.org.uk (accessed 13 Dec. 2015).
69   HAS, AG9/48; *Kelly's Dir. Herefs.* (1917); *Tilleys Ledbury Almanack* (1961, 1973, 1976).
70   TNA, RG 11/2581; RG 12/2051.

Cider retailing was established at Staplow, close to the canal wharf, by 1851, and the Oak Inn opened there before 1871.[71] The publican in 1881 and 1891 also worked as a blacksmith; his successor between 1901 and 1917 as a carpenter.[72] William Bishop, previously at The Old Country, was trading at Staplow in 1926.[73] The pub was still open in 2015.

The Poor

Charities

It was reported in 1547 that Sir Rowland Morton had given the parish a house and 4 a. of land, the revenue from which was to be used for the poor. There is no later record of the charity, unless it became part of the poor's land.[74]

In the 16th and 17th centuries several bequests provided doles and gifts for the poor of Bosbury.[75] In 1750 a number of such small sums were used to buy land in Catley Rye meadow from James Walwyn of Longworth in Lugwardine.[76] William Nash, by indenture dated 1751, conveyed to trustees a rent-charge from land at Baggin's Hill, Ledbury, to buy bread for the Bosbury poor. An unknown donor augmented the charity with a rent charge on part of the Gold Hill estate. Monies were being collected and disbursed from these in the 1830s. Both charities had ceased to operate by 2008.[77]

In 1670, John Powell left £20 for building and erecting almshouses. There is no record of it, but the money was presumably applied for this purpose for in the 18th century a workhouse was established next to the almshouses.[78]

Several members of the Brydges family of Old Colwall, who held extensive lands in Bosbury,[79] left money to provide clothing for the Bosbury poor. Income from £200 left by William Brydges in 1704 was supplemented by £50 from each of William and Elizabeth Brydges.[80] The clothing was distributed from Old Colwall until its sale in the early 19th century to James Martin. In 1842, after a long dispute, Martin's offer of the sum of £150 capital as well as interest for the period 1827–42 was accepted. Parish records show collection and disbursement of monies from the bread and clothing endowed charities

71   TNA, HO 107/1975; TNA, RG 10/2681; *Lascelles Dir. Herefs.* (1851); *Littlebury's Dir. Herefs.* (1867).
72   TNA, RG 11/2581, RG 12/2051, RG 13/2470; *Kelly's Dir. Herefs,* (1917).
73   TNA, RG 13/2470; *Kelly's Dir Herefs.* (1926).
74   TNA, E 301/24, transcribed in HCA, 6450/2, p. 27; Bentley, *Hist. Bosbury* (1891), 50.
75   TNA, PROB 11/428 will of John Harford, 1559; PROB 11/76 will of William Wood, 1590; PROB 11/78 will of Anthony Washbourne, 1591; PROB 11/152 will of William Bridge, 1627; PROB 11/249 will of William Pullen, 1655; PROB 11/309 will of Anthony Turner, 1662; HAS, 14/1/11, will of John Danford 1572; 6/3/24 will of Thomas Barclay 1572; 43/1/64 will of John Watkins 1580; 45/4/76 will of James Woodyatt, 1597; 58/1/5 will of Thomas Danett 1677.
76   Indenture of 1750, http://www.bosburyhistoryresource.org.uk (accessed 2 Jan. 2016).
77   *Rpts of the Commissioners for inquiring concerning Charities* (1819–1837), 100–102: copy in HAS library; Par. Rec., charity rec.; http://www.charitycommission.gov.uk (accessed 18 Dec. 2015).
78   TNA, PROB 11/334, will of John Powell, 1670; TNA, C 93/37/25; below, Poor Relief.
79   Above, Land Ownership.
80   TNA, PROB 11/479, will of William Brydges of Colwall, 1704.

after this date.[81] The charity was augmented by Robert Probert by will of 1860. In 1891 eight men received coats.[82] Efforts made to claim a bequest from the estate of another Elizabeth Brydges in the 1830s at first failed, but the bread charity was operating in 1891.[83] Both charities had ceased to operate by 2008 when they were removed from the register.[84]

Francis Brydges (d. 1727) bequeathed £100 to buy land, the profits from which were to be used to apprentice boys or girls born in Bosbury. Land was bought at Noverings. Accounts were not kept until 1830; after 1835 the vicar managed the fund.[85] Surviving indentures show that the charity apprenticed girls and boys to a variety of trades between 1834 and 1904.[86] In 1923 a revised scheme was approved which relaxed the residence requirements for applicants and amended the objects to 'helping the advancement of young people'. By 1958 there were difficulties in disbursing money from the charity, then called Noverings Apprenticeship charity, and in 2008 it was removed from the register as no longer operational.[87]

In 1964 the charities of Ann Jenkins, Elizabeth Brydges, Francis Brydges, William Brydges, William Nash and the Poor's Land were each registered under the working name Bosbury Church Charities.[88] Balances were £326 in 1966; between then and 1984 vouchers were disbursed to parishioners on St Thomas's Day. A grant of £75 was given to an apprentice to buy books in 1984.[89] The charities were removed from the register as inoperative in 2008.[90]

A subscription clothing charity ran from 1861 to 1870 with annual income between £50 and £74. Members' subscriptions, of between 1*d*. and 4*d*., were augmented by a small number of donations. A similar charity to provide subsidised coal ran from 1848 to 1862; in 1865–6 income and expenditure were £27 4s 10*d*. A further charity, to subsidise coal for large families, was started by the wife of J.H. Underwood, vicar 1830–56; it was still going in 1857.[91]

81 Par. Rec., vestry min., vol. 2, pp. 332–3; charities account bk. 1836–1906; accounts for subscription charities; coal charity accounts 1848–1862.
82 Bentley, *Hist. Bosbury* (1891), 50–1.
83 TNA, PROB 11/1462, will of Elizabeth Brydges 1804; *Rpts of the Commissioners for inquiring concerning Charities* (1819 –37), 98–101: copy in HAS library; Bentley, *Hist. Bosbury* (1891), 51.
84 http://www.charitycommission.gov.uk (accessed 18 Dec. 2015).
85 *Rpts of the Commissioners for inquiring concerning Charities* (1819–1837), 100; Par. Rec., charities account bk. 1836–1906.
86 http://www.bosburyhistoryresource.org.uk/bosbury-apprentices (accessed 6 Nov. 2015).
87 Par. Rec., vestry min. vol. 4, 18 Apr. 1922, 3 Apr. 1923, 6 Apr. 1920, 8 Apr. 1958; http://www. charitycommission.gov.uk (accessed 18 Dec. 2015).
88 http://apps.charitycommission.gov.uk, record for Bosbury Church Charities (accessed 17 Dec. 2015).
89 Par. Rec., vestry mins., vol. 4, 12 Apr. 1966, 3 Apr. 1984.
90 Par. Rec., vestry mins. vol. 4, 18 Apr. 1922, 3 Apr. 1923, 6 Apr. 1920, 8 Apr. 1958; http://www. charitycommission.gov.uk (accessed 18 Dec. 2015).
91 Par. Rec., charities account bk. 1836–1906; Par. Rec., accounts for subscription charities; Par. Rec., coal charity accounts 1848–62; Par. Rec., vestry min., vol. 4, Dec. 1857.

Poor Relief Before 1834

The vestry, at its regular meetings, oversaw poor relief under the old poor law. In April 1749 weekly doles of between 1s. and 2s. were paid to 13 paupers. In April 1757 weekly pay to 20 paupers totalled £1 7s. 8d. In 1797 loaves were distributed to the poor who did not receive poor relief, while in 1799 coal was distributed by James Hartland of Temple Court.[92]

In 1741 the vestry agreed to pay £1 10s. a year for a house for the use of the parish poor. Members considered using Ledbury workhouse in 1752, and agreed to do so in 1757. In 1763 the contract was changed to Hereford workhouse.[93] In 1767 work spinning hemp and flax was provided for the poor within the parish.[94] The following year an agreement was made with a master at Ledbury, but in 1770 the contract was again placed with Hereford. In 1776 it was reported that there was no workhouse in the parish and out relief of £112 12s. 3d. had been paid. The following year it was decided to erect a workhouse beside the almshouses in Bosbury. The contract was let for £120 a year in 1784.[95] The parish retained the workhouse until 1837 when it was sold.[96]

Between 1692 and 1829 the vestry arranged apprenticeships for pauper children.[97] By 1772 allocations were made by lot. In 1796 poor children aged between 10 and 13 were allocated to farmers and freeholders in the parish, normally for a term of five years. The system was discontinued in 1829 when all current indentures were cancelled.[98] By the early 1830s apprenticeships were being funded from the Francis Brydges charity (above).

Ledbury or Hereford surgeons were paid to treat the poor, as in 1749 when Edmund Powell was engaged to treat Martha Hall's leg for 1 guinea, or 2 guineas for 'a perfect cure'. Richard Hill of Ledbury was to be paid £8 in 1761 but the payment was later disputed. 'Mr Hardwicke' from Hereford was paid 4 guineas to cure a patient in 1768.[99] Between 1753 and 1758 the vestry paid a subscription of £1 1s. to Worcester Infirmary.[100]

At times the vestry took steps to control costs: paupers without a legal settlement were removed, and some applications for relief were refused.[101] By the 1820s subsidised coal was provided for the poor. Relief was administered separately for Bosbury and Upleadon. Expenditure for 1820 was £220 4s. 5½d. for Bosbury and £260 7s. 9½d. for Upleadon.[102]

Under the New Poor Law, Bosbury became part of Ledbury Poor Law Union from 1834.[103]

---

92   Par. Rec., vestry min., vol. 1, Apr. 1749, Apr. 1757; vol. 2, pp. 24, 43 (undated).
93   Par. Rec., vestry min., vol. 1, Feb. 1741, June 1752; 31 March 1757, Apr. 1763, Apr. 1770.
94   Par. Rec., vestry min., vol. 1, June 1767.
95   Par. Rec., vestry min., vol. 1, Aug. 1768, Apr. 1770, Sept. 1776, Feb. 1784.
96   Par. Rec., vestry min., vol. 3, Aug. 1837.
97   See for example, the agreement of 1701 between Robert Barkley and the Bosbury churchwardens to take John Ward as apprentice: http://www.bosburyhistoryresource.org.uk (accessed 13 Dec. 2015).
98   Par. Rec., vestry min., vol. 1, 9 Feb. 1772, vol. 2, 18 Feb. 1796, vol. 3, 4 Aug. 1829.
99   Par. Rec., vestry min., vol. 1, Oct. 1749, Oct. 1761, Dec. 1761, Dec. 1768.
100 Par. Rec., vestry min., vol. 1, Apr. 1753, Apr., Aug. 1757.
101 Par. Rec., vestry min., vol. 2, Dec. 1820, Apr. 1846 (removal of a pauper to Abergavenny).
102 Par. Rec., vestry min., vol. 2, Nov. 1825, May 1821.
103 http://www.workhouses.org.uk/Ledbury (accessed 19 May 2016).

Education

Boys' Grammar School

In 1548 it was reported that Richard 'Poyke' (Powick) at an unknown date had conveyed to Richard Hope and others land and other stock producing 58s. 4½d. a year, which had 'always' been used to pay a schoolmaster. Hope may have been the man of that name who lived in the parish in the 1520s. Thomas Kylling or Keyling, 'a man of good conversation and learning' had been schoolmaster for four or five years; his duties included teaching the boys to play the organ.[104] A further endowment in 1565 or 1566 provided a stipend of £8 4s. 2d., charged on Wormbridge manor, to the Bosbury schoolmaster, who was to be a clergyman.[105]

Masters were appointed regularly in the 17th and 18th centuries. Among them were several Bosbury vicars including George Wall (d. 1641), his successor William Coke, Joshua Elmhurst (appointed 1684 before he became vicar) and John Jones (d. 1748).[106] Some were not so well qualified, and in 1800 the vicar and others brought a suit in Chancery alleging misconduct and neglect of duty against trustees appointed in 1781. Joseph Thomas, appointed schoolmaster in 1798, was said to be neither a clergyman nor a graduate but 'an illiterate man, of disreputable character' who had twice been declared bankrupt. It was claimed that two pieces of charity land had been lost and that the trustees had let other lands to each other at less than the market rent. The schoolhouse was apparently in 'a dilapidated and ruinous state' between 1798 and 1812, when the trustees were ordered to appoint a new master. The parochial return for 1819, while noting the alleged misconduct, recorded the free grammar school served 20–25 children.[107] In 1835, it having been reported that there had been no schoolmaster for 12 years, the school room was shut up, and that as the charity was useless to parishioners, the assets were conveyed to the vicar, J.H. Underwood, and 12 other trustees.[108]

The new trustees put repairs in hand and appointed a schoolmaster at a salary of £40. The school reopened in 1838, open to all children born to Bosbury couples who were married, did not receive parish relief, and paid taxes.[109] The new trustees also administered John Meaking's bequest, made in 1811, of £100, the income of which was to be used to pay half-guinea rewards to the best scholars in Latin and English prose

---

104 TNA, E 301/25, copied in HCA, 6450/2; E 301/24; *Cal. Pat. Edw. VI* 1549–51, 28; 1548; for Hope, see above this section. It would appear that the gift of Sir Rowland Morton of the Grange, who came to be credited with the foundation of the grammar school, was in fact for the poor.

105 For the early history of the school see N. Carlisle, *A concise description of the endowed grammar schools of England and Wales*, I (London, 1818), 480–2; *Digest of Returns Select Cttee on the Education of the Poor*, HC 224 (1819) ix (1), 332.

106 e.g. HAS, AL19/18, f. 182v.; AL19/20, f. 28; Bentley, *Hist. Bosbury* (1891), 46.

107 Carlisle, *Concise description of endowed grammar schools*, I, 480–2; *Digest of Returns Select Cttee on the Education of the Poor*, HC 224 (1819) ix (1), 332.

108 *Digest of Returns Select Cttee on the Education of the Poor*, (1819) ix (1), 332; *Abstract of Answers and Returns relative to the State of Education in England*, HC 62 (1835), xli, xiii. *Rpts of the Commissioners for inquiring concerning Charities* (1819–1837), 96–98: copy in HAS libr.

109 Grammar school records, http://www.bosburyhistoryresource.org.uk (accessed 17 Aug. 2015).

Figure 17 *The former Boys' Grammar School, 2015.*

and verse composition, and in arithmetic. The funds had earlier been misapplied in providing clothing.[110]

In 1841 the vicar J.H. Underwood was confirmed headmaster and a second master appointed. Increased numbers attending the school led to the introduction of the monitorial system in 1847. A weekly payment of 1*d.* per child was introduced in 1857 as charity income was insufficient to cover the costs of a certificated schoolmaster.[111]

By 1862 the school was a National School.[112] In 1886 it had 91 places with average attendance of 40. An annual grant of £37 was received. [113] In 1893 average attendance was just over 50. Income was then £176 11*s.* 8*d.*, comprising the endowment of £90, annual grant of £53, fee grant of £27 9*s.* and other income of £4 2*s.* 6*d.*[114]

A new scheme of administration for the Grammar School and the Meaking's Charity was approved by the Charity Commissioners in 1891. The new foundation was conducted as a Public Elementary School. Prizes worth £3 were to be given annually.[115] Schemes of 1957 and 1973 authorised the charity to assist young people in Bosbury with their educational needs. In 2015 the Bosbury Educational Foundation continued to give grants towards the cost of higher education to young people who had lived in the parish for at least three years. In 2014 the charity's income was £22,233 and expenditure was £6,313.[116]

110 *Rpts of the Commissioners for inquiring concerning Charities* (1819–37), 100.
111 Grammar school records, http://www.bosburyhistoryresource.org.uk (accessed 17 Aug. 2015).
112 *Rpt of the Cttee of Council on Education* [3007] HC (1862) xlii.
113 *Rpt of the Cttee of Council on Education (England and Wales); with appendix 1885–6* [C. 4849–I] HC (1886), xxiv.
114 *Returns relating to Elementary Education, 1893* [C. 7529] HC (1894), lxv.
115 HAS, R95/52/7, *Bosbury Grammar School Scheme 1890.*
116 The Bosbury Educational Foundation, charity no. 527140, http://apps.charitycommission.gov.uk (accessed 13 Dec. 2015).

The grammar school building stands in the north-east corner of the churchyard, adjoining the gate-house range of Old Court on the north. The oldest remaining part of the building is the west wall, timber-framed with brick in-fill, which is of the 17th century; the other walls were largely rebuilt, or at least refaced, in brick c.1880.[117]

Other Schools

In addition to the grammar school, the parochial return for 1819 recorded three dame schools in different parts of the parish teaching a total of 32 children.[118] In 1835 one school taught 30 boys and five girls, paid for by their parents. A Sunday school was established at the parish church in 1829, and taught 40 boys and 45 girls in 1835. The Wesleyans also ran a Sunday school, with 12 children.[119]

Girls' School

In 1848 the trustees of the Grammar School conveyed land opposite the churchyard for the construction of a National School for girls 'of the labouring and manufacturing and other poorer classes'.[120] The building opened in 1849; its Bath stone north window with 'handsome mullions', and barge-board with alternate trefoil and acorn decoration were said to give 'a handsome finish to the village front'.[121] In 1862 it received a government grant of £118 10s.[122]

In 1860 the income of the Girls' School was £52 4s. 1d., mainly from donations with £13 4s. 11d. raised from 'school pence'. In 1875 income was £52 12s. 10d., including a government grant of £17 17s. 9d. and school pence of £6 9s. 7d.[123] By 1892–3 the school received an annual grant of £49 15s., fee grant of £31 1s. 8d., endowment income of £3 and voluntary contributions of £41 12s. 6d.[124] The school had 45 pupils in 1871.[125] By 1885/6 it was a Girls' and Infants' school with accommodation for 106 and average attendance of 77.[126] In 1901 its capacity was 118, average attendance 69.[127]

Education after 1902

The responsibilities of the Herefordshire Education Authority, established in 1902, included the approval of grants for premises and appointment of teachers. Plans to improve accommodation at the Bosbury schools, among them rebuilding the boys'

117 RCHM, *Herefordshire*, ii. 20; Brooks and Pevsner, *Herefordshire*, 117.
118 *Digest of Returns Select Cttee on the Education of the Poor*, HC 224 (1819) ix (i), 332.
119 *Returns relating to Elementary Education, 1835*, HC 62 (1835), xli, xlii.
120 Bosbury Grammar School, Mins of Trustees Meeting 15 May 1848, http://www.bosburyhistory resource.org.uk (accessed 17 Aug. 2015); TNA, C 54/13702, 1205991848, conveyance of 24 June, 1848 (another copy in the Par. Rec.).
121 *Hereford Jnl*, 28 Feb. 1849, transcript, http://www.bosburyhistoryresource.org.uk (accessed 22 Aug. 2015).
122 *Rpt of the Cttee of Council on Education; with appendix 1862*, HC (1862), xlii (i).
123 Par. Rec., subscription charities account bk. 1857–79.
124 *Returns Relating to Elementary Education, 1893*. [C. 7529] HC (1894) lxv.
125 *Rpt of the Cttee of Council on Education 1871*, HC 201 (1871), lv.32.
126 *Rpt of the Cttee of Council on Education (England and Wales); with appendix 1885–86*, HC (1886), xxiv.
127 *Schools in Receipt of Parliamentary Grants 1900–1*. [Cd. 703] HC (1901), lv.

school on the opposite side of the road, were discussed before 1914. The old grammar school building was modified in 1911, creating two separate classrooms and a lobby for the external door, with improved heating and lighting. The following year the younger boys were moved from the Girls' and Infants' School and a new Infant teacher appointed to teach them.[128]

The raising of the school leaving age to 14 in 1918 and concern about appropriate training for older children stimulated further plans for reorganisation. In 1920 Robert Buchanan offered £1,500 towards provision of technical education and a further £3,000 towards a new school, but nothing was done before his death later that year. An alternative scheme, developed by the LEA in 1922, to amalgamate the schools was blocked by school managers. Only the appointment of a headmistress for the Boys' School, a cost cutting measure, went ahead. The school received a favourable inspection report in 1931. In 1936 there were concerns that some Bosbury children were being sent to schools outside the parish.[129]

In 1939 the LEA proposed closing the Boys' School and providing a mixed school for juniors and infants on the Girls' School premises.[130] The increase in the school leaving age to 15 under the 1944 Education Act led to a modified scheme to provide secondary education for pupils over 11 in the Boys' School premises.[131] In 1949 secondary education in the village closed, and the older children moved to Ashperton Primary School, except for girls transferred to Ledbury. Bosbury Boys' School ceased to be recognised as a separate school from 1950, although the premises continued to be used by the combined Junior and Infant school.[132] In 1965 60 junior pupils were being taught there although the building had no electricity or hot water.[133] The school closed in 1968.[134]

A new school with four classrooms, one for infants and three for juniors opened in September 1968 on a site behind the old Girls' School buildings, which were demolished. Children from Fromes Hill were moved there in 1976 on the closure of their school.[135]

In 2014 Bosbury Church of England Primary School achieved the grade 'Outstanding' in its Ofsted report. The school had capacity for 140 pupils with 124 on the roll.[136] The closest secondary school to Bosbury was in Ledbury.

---

128 HAS, B61/82, 10 Sept. 1908; B61/83, 11 March 1911, B61/83, 15 June 1912; Par. Rec., boys' school managers' min. bk. 1906–1946, 21 July 1911, 10 May, 14 Aug. 1912.

129 Par. Rec., boys' school managers' min. bk. 1906–46, 24 Jan., 12 Feb., 7 May 1920, 15 May 1922, 5 Nov. 1931, 29 Jan. 1936.

130 Par. Rec., managers' min. bk. 1906–46, 24 Nov. 1939.

131 Par. Rec., Letter from A.P. Whitehead, Director Education, Hereford, to Revd A. Orton, Bosbury Vicarage, 22 Nov. 1944.

132 HAS, D87/89, 28 May, 24 Sept. 1949, 22 Sept. 1951.

133 *Hereford Evening News*, 20 Jan. 1965, http://www.bosburyhistoryresource.org.uk (accessed 6 Dec. 2015).

134 Par. Rec., Bosbury educational foundation min. bk., 5 July 1968.

135 HAS, AD32/277; Par. Rec., parochial church council min., 1937 onwards. 17 May 1976.

136 Bosbury Church of England primary school, http://www.bosburyprimaryschool.co.uk (accessed 17 Aug. 2015).

RELIGIOUS HISTORY

Parochial Organisation

The surviving 11th-century or earlier tub font, discovered in 1844 buried beneath the floor at the west end of the church, indicates that there was an Anglo-Saxon church in Bosbury, and in 1086 a priest held one hide of land on the bishop's manor.[1] The size of the endowment implies that the church was an important one, but its position immediately south of the bishop's manor house suggests an origin as a manorial church. The parish was probably originally served from the mother church of Ledbury.[2] The bishop of Hereford has been patron of the living since the early Middle Ages.

There was no change in the ecclesiastical parish or its boundaries until the later 20th century. From 1959 Bosbury was held in plurality with Coddington and Wellington Heath. In 1982 the benefice of Bosbury and Wellington Heath was united to that of Stretton Grandison with Ashperton and Canon Frome.[3] In 1998 Bosbury became part of the Ledbury Team Ministry; it remained so in 2015, as part of the Hop Churches group.[4]

Endowment

In 1243 the pope granted the bishop permission to appropriate the rectory 'to the charges of [food for] his table', but the permission was not acted upon until after a second papal grant in 1276, when Bishop Cantilupe was allowed to appropriate the rectory at the next vacancy, appointing a vicar with an appropriate income. A vicar was first recorded in 1278.[5] In 1291 the bishop received £20 from the church, presumably the value of the rectory, and the vicar £4 13s. 4d., presumably from the small tithes as there is no record of any vicarial glebe. Before 1496 'Thomas late bishop of Hereford', presumably Thomas Myllyng (bishop 1474–92), augmented the vicarage by a grant of the hay tithe of Catley, valued at 20s. a year. By the early 16th century the value of the vicarage had risen to £10 a year, and in 1554 to £10 3s. 9d.[6] In the early 17th century John Scudamore, Viscount Scudamore, owner of Upleadon manor, gave the great tithes of Catley (which

1   R. Bryant and M. Hare, *Corpus of Anglo-Saxon Stone Sculpture: the West Midlands* X (London, 2012), 383–4; *Domesday*, 502.
2   S.K. Waddington, 'The Anglo-Saxon mother churches of eastern Herefordshire', *TWNFC*, 62 (2014), 76–7.
3   Par. Rec., PCC min. bk. 1937–65, 3 Nov. 1959; *The Times*, 23 Nov. 1982, from Times Digital Archive, accessed 26 Oct. 2015.
4   Crockford, *Clerical Dir.* (2000/1), s.v. Susan Strutt, team vicar; http://www.ledburyparishchurch.org.uk/teammin.html (accessed 12 May 2016); inf. from Hereford diocesan office.
5   *Cal. Papal Regs*, i. 202; *Reg. Cantilupe*, 126, 307.
6   *Taxatio Ecclesiastica* (Rec. Com. 1802), 160; HAS, AM33/13; *Reg. Mayew*, 235; HCA, 5602/11.

had belonged to the Hospitallers) to the vicar and his successors.[7] The vicar's tithes were commuted for a rent charge of £400 a year in 1836.[8] In 1867, however, the gross income of the living was said to be only £393.[9] In 1881 the Ecclesiastical Commissioners augmented the living with c.6 a. of land adjoining the vicarage house, but even so it was worth only £240 net in the early 20th century.[10]

There is no evidence for the position of the vicarage house until 1840 when it lay immediately west of the church, in the Bosbury division of the parish.[11] In 1665 the vicar, William Coke, was assessed for tax on four hearths in a house in Upleadon, perhaps his private house. When he died in 1690 the house or that part of it in his occupation, comprised a study, parlour, kitchen, hall, and toploft.[12] In 1716 and 1719 the vicar lived in the vicarage house, presumably the one beside the church, which was in good repair. The vicar J.E. Cheese added a new wing in 1867, to designs by George Haddon of Hereford.[13] The house was sold in 1906, and replaced by one built in 1907, to designs of Joseph Farmer, on land about half a mile east of the village given by W.B. Mynors of Bosbury House.[14] That house was sold in 1968 and renamed Great Gables; a new vicarage house, built on part of its garden, still belonged to the diocese in 2015.[15]

Pastoral Care and Religious Life

The Middle Ages

Two priests, possibly rectors, of Bosbury, Edulph and Ralph, witnessed deeds at different times in the mid 12th century.[16] The two known medieval rectors were both royal nominees, presented during vacancies in the see of Hereford. In 1200 King John presented his priest Master Swan, whose title suggests he may have been a university graduate. Master Simon de Baledon, a king's clerk presented by Henry III in 1269, was a member of Oxford University. He became a canon of Lichfield and an official of the bishop of Coventry and Lichfield in 1275, and it seems unlikely that he spent much, if any, time in Bosbury.[17]

7   Bentley, *Hist. Bosbury* (1891), 10–11, citing a special Act of Parliament.
8   TNA, IR 29/14 (tithe apportionment): http://www.bosburyhistoryresource.org.uk (accessed 26 Oct. 2015).
9   HAS, HD10/23: Diocesan Year Boxes 1866.
10   Bentley, *Hist. Bosbury* (1891), 11; *Kelly's Dir. Herefs.* (1913).
11   G. Gwatkin, 'Bosbury Tithe Map'.
12   HAS Libr., typescript transcript of 1665 hearth tax by J. Harnden, p. 83; HAS, 110/3/3, will of William Coke, priest, 1690.
13   HAS, HD5/14/25, 100; *Hereford Times*, 19 Oct. 1867.
14   HAS, AA61/33; OS map, 1:10560, 1926 edn, http://www.bosburyhistoryresource.org.uk (accessed 10 Sept. 2015).
15   HAS, B37/1; HAS, AA61/33 – sale particulars, May 1968; Brooks and Pevsner, *Herefordshire*, 118; local inf.
16   J. Barrow (ed.), *English Episcopal Acta*, vii: *Hereford 1079–1234* (London, 1993), nos 28. 116.
17   T.D. Hardy (ed.), *Rotuli Chartarum* (Rec. Comm., 1837) i (1), 75; *Cal Pat. 1266–72*, 321; *Emden, Oxf. Univ. Reg. to 1500*, i. 98–9.

The income of the vicarage established *c*.1278 was too low, at least until its augmentation in the late 15th century, to attract well-educated or ambitious men. None of the 23 recorded vicars presented between 1279 and 1472 is known to have been a university graduate, although Walter of Malvern, vicar *c*.1300, was given the title 'dominus', and William Odingley in 1468 the title 'Sir', both used for men with a bachelor's degree.[18] Four vicars resigned, and another four exchanged, the living; one in 1364, after only one year. Three vicars were presented in quick succession in 1349, the year of the Black Death: John de Herwynton in June on the death of the previous vicar, Richard de Brugge in July on the death of Herwynton, and Philip Smith in September.[19] Some vicars, on the other hand, served many years: William Toby, presented in 1302, only resigned in 1321; David ap Kynwerit, presented in 1400, was still vicar in 1418 when he witnessed a parishioner's will, and Richard Oldbury served from 1439 to 1458.[20]

Four late 15th- and earlier 16th-century vicars were given the title Sir and one the title Master, but none can be certainly identified as graduates of Oxford or Cambridge. Thomas Fowler, who resigned the living in 1508, had been appointed titular bishop of 'Lachorens' in 1505 and was presumably already acting as assistant bishop in Hereford diocese while he was at Bosbury.[21] Roger Walker, presented in 1508, was accused of 'incontinence' in 1512, but continued to hold the living until his death in 1517.[22]

At least some vicars were assisted by chaplains. In 1279 both the vicar and a chaplain appeared as witnesses in a suit before the bishop. Richard Sterre, chaplain, accused of fornication with a Bosbury woman in 1397 and apparently then living in the parish, had been chaplain of Cradley.[23] Robert Roge of Bosbury, a chaplain in the diocese in 1436, may have served in the parish, perhaps at a chantry or other chapel within the church. Sir Thomas Ward, whose will in 1446 was witnessed by the vicar, seems to have been another chaplain.[24] At least some of these chaplains may have been employed for the 'the service of the Virgin Mary' although that service was not recorded until 1544 when a parishioner owed it two cows which was presumably part of its endowment.[25] The only recorded chantry in the church was the one, of unknown dedication, founded by Thomas Morton, archdeacon of Hereford, in 1510.[26] In 1529 the chantry priest, Robert Bartlet, increased the priest's stipend by a rent of 20*s*. a year.[27] The licence for the foundation provided for an endowment of lands worth up to £10 a year, but if the rents of 58*s*. 4½*d*. held by the church in 1547 were from this chantry, its endowment fell far short of that sum.[28]

18 *Reg. Swinfield*, 401; Faraday (ed.), *Cal. Hereford Probate and Admin. Acts 1407–1550*, 54.
19 *Reg. Lewis Charlton*, 71; *Reg. Trillek*, 376, 377, 380.
20 *Reg. Swinfield*, 533; *Reg. Orleton*, 201; *Reg. Trefnant*, 184; *Reg. Spofford*, 362; *Reg. Stanbury*, 175; Faraday (ed.), *Cal. Hereford Probate and Admin. Acts 1407–1550*, 2.
21 *Reg Mayew*, 275; http://www.catholic-hierarchy.org (accessed 29 Aug. 2015).
22 *Reg. Mayew*, 143, 276, 281.
23 *Reg. Cantilupe*, 197; A.T. Bannister, 'Visitation Returns of the Diocese of Hereford in 1397', *EHR*, xlv (1930), 95.
24 *Reg. Spofford*, 211; *Cal. Probate & Admin. Acts*, Faraday, 15.
25 HAS, 23/1/2, will of John Hope, 1544.
26 *L & P Hen VIII*, I, p. 364.
27 HCA, Transcript of Chapter Act Book, by P.G.S. Baylis, I, no. 333; *Fasti Ecclesiae Anglicanae 1300–1541*, http://www.british-history.ac.uk (accessed 29 Aug. 2015).
28 *The Herefordshire Chantry Valuations of 1547*, M.A. Faraday (ed.) (2012), 25.

The only recorded statues in the medieval church were those of the Virgin Mary at the church door and of St Erasmus, before which wax tapers were burnt in 1513. By 1496 the bishop was providing oil for another light, before the high altar of the church.[29]

Because the manor house was a favourite residence of many medieval bishops, Bosbury church was occasionally used for ordinations and visitations. A visitation was held there in 1345. Ordinations were held in the church at Easter 1349, during the Black Death, and in 1449. Another took place in the bishop's chapel, presumably within the manor house, in 1368.[30] That chapel was first recorded in 1293 when it was repaired. In 1322, for unknown reasons, a man attacked an acolyte during a service there.[31]

The Templars and the Hospitallers had a chapel in Upleadon, in their manor house or preceptory.[32] It appears to have had some parochial functions: in 1505 the tenant of the manor house was responsible for finding a chaplain to serve the chapel and the tenant of the Nelmes had to provide 2 lb. wax for use there.[33] In 1521 the bishop complained that the prior's tenant had either built a new 'oratory' or restored an old one, and had placed a 'foreign' priest in it; moreover he had added a baptistery and erected a tomb for himself, his wife and family, thus implying that the chapel had rights of baptism and burial. The prior responded that the inhabitants of Upleadon had never been obliged to attend Bosbury church, and he and his predecessors had the right to administer the sacraments to them. The outcome of the dispute is unknown, but in 1545 'all oblations arising from a chapel in Bosbury lately belonging to the hospital' were among the assets of Temple Court manor.[34] The chapel was not recorded again and presumably fell out of use soon afterwards.

From the Reformation to the 19th Century

Thomas Blockley, who was serving the church by 1546 although he did not become vicar until 1547, stayed throughout the reigns of Edward VI and Mary, dying *c.*1558. A former monk of Worcester, he was 'an impotent old man' in 1554.[35] He witnessed parishioners' wills in 1546 and 1556.[36] During his incumbency some old ways continued. As late as 1546 one parishioner left 3*s.* 4*d.* to a priest to pray for her husband's soul; another left 10*s.* to the vicar and another named priest to pray for him, as well as a cow to the stock of the parish church to pay a priest to pray for him and for all Christian souls. In 1557, a parishioner left 12*d.* to 'the canopy over the blessed sacrament of the High Altar', presumably towards buying one to re-equip the church for Catholic worship under Mary.[37]

---

29   TNA, PROB 11/17, will of William Wooding, 1513; HAS, AM33/13; HAS, O43.
30   *Reg. Trillek*, 30, 495; *Reg. Beauchamp*, 13; *Reg. Lewis Charlton*, 116.
31   HCA, R366; *Reg. Orleton*, 245.
32   TNA, E 199/18/4; Larking (ed.), *Knights Hospitallers in England* (Camden Soc., 1857), 195.
33   HAS, A63/III/23/1, ff. 7v., 9v.
34   *Reg. Bothe*, 87–8, 90–1; TNA, E 368/319.
35   HAS, 2/1/32, will of Cicely Woodyatt, 1546; A.T. Bannister, *Diocese of Hereford Institutions 1539–1900*, 6; Faraday (ed.), *Cal. Hereford Probate and Admin. Acts 1407–1550*, 326; TNA, E 178/3218; HCA, 5602/11.
36   HAS, 2/1/32, will of Cecily Woodyatt 1546; 32/1/12 will of Richard Nash 1556; 31/2/14, will of William Mutlow, 1556.
37   HAS, 2/1/32, will of Cicely Woodyatt 1546; 2/4/32, will of Thomas Brown, 1546; 5/1/18, will of Roger Alcock, 1557.

Blockley's successor James ap Price was appointed overseer of parishioners' wills in 1559 and 1572, and received legacies, one of a black horse, from other parishioners in 1567 and 1571; he witnessed several wills, the last in 1583.[38] His successor was appointed in 1588, but Price was apparently still living in the parish in 1588 when William Wood made his will leaving 'Sir James Price late vicar of Bosbury' 3s. 4d. for tithe forgotten. Other aspects of Wood's will demonstrate conservatism if not recusancy: he asked for the prayers of 'our blessed Lady Saint Mary the mother of God and our saviour Jesus Christ and all the patriarchs and prophets the holy apostles martyrs confessors and virgins and all the blessed company of heaven'. In 1592, two years after his death, he was listed as a recusant.[39] By contrast, John Mutlow (d. 1607), whose daughters were called Mercy, Truth and Comfort, seems to have held Puritan views. Those views were probably more in accord with those of the vicar who was accused in 1595 of failing to wear the surplice, even when administering communion on Whit Sunday, and of omitting some prayers from services.[40]

George Wall, an Oxford graduate, served the church for 33 years, from 1608 or 1609 until his death in 1641, holding Rous Lench, Worcs., in plurality from 1616 to 1640.[41] He lived in Bosbury most if not all the time, being mentioned in the wills of several parishioners. One of them, William Bridge, in 1627 included 'our vicar Mr Wall' and his wife among the six guests to be invited to his funeral dinner, a week after his burial.[42] Relations with other parishioners were less cordial: in 1621 Wall brought a suit against James Powell to recover tithe from Lower Mill.[43] Wall's own will, dated 1641, suggests a moderate Puritanism. He commended his soul 'into the sure protection of my most blessed lord and saviour Jesus Christ, whom I have found a most merciful comforter in subduing the enemy of my salvation and all the fiery darts of his temptations', and asked to be buried in the chancel of Bosbury church.[44]

William Coke, son of George Coke, bishop of Hereford 1636–46, was vicar by 1655,[45] and was probably Wall's immediate successor. He also held the prebend of Barton Colwall from 1645. He appears to have remained at Bosbury throughout the Interregnum: when in 1660 he lobbied, unsuccessfully, for a prebend at Worcester, he referred to his father's sufferings, but said nothing about any sufferings of his own.[46] Coke witnessed Bosbury wills in 1660 and 1661, and received a legacy from a Bosbury yeoman in 1662, but from 1665 he may have spent part of his time in Bromyard where

38   HAS, 24/2/8, will of Hugh Hill 1559; 14/1/11, will of John Danford, 1572; 26/4/25, will of John Knight, 1567; 21/2/36, will of Thomas Hall, 1571; 3/5/16, will of John Finch, 1583.
39   TNA, PROB 11/76, will of William Wood, 1590; *Cal. Cecil Papers in Hatfield House*, IV (HMC, 1892), http://www.british-history.ac.uk/cal-cecil-papers/vol4/pp249-277 (accessed 5 Aug. 2014).
40   HAS, 9/2/42, will of John Mutlow, 1607; HAS, HD4/1/156 [unfoliated and undated].
41   A.T. Bannister, *Diocese of Hereford Institutions 1539–1900*: MS note in Hereford cathedral library copy; Par. Rec., burials; Foster, *Alumni Oxonienses*, s.v. Wall, George; http://www.theclergydatabase.org.uk (accessed 23 Oct. 2015).
42   HAS, 16/4/17, will of Richard Finch the elder, 1613; 331/1/7, will of John Pullen, 1626; TNA, PROB 11/165, will of William Price, 1634; PROB 11/152, will of William Bridge, 1627.
43   HAS, AL19/16, pp. 249–50.
44   HAS, 54/2/21, will of George Wall, 1641.
45   TNA, PROB 11/264 will of Richard Bacon, 1655; PROB 11/249 will of William Pullen, 1655.
46   A.G. Matthews, *Walker Revised*, 192; *Cal. SP Dom.*, 1660–1, 252; F.T. Havergal, *Fasti Herefordenses*, 61; http://www.theclergydatabase.org.uk, s.v. William Coke (accessed 23 Oct. 2015).

he held one of the three portions of the rectory.[47] Benjamin Bateman, ordained priest in 1687 to serve the cure of Bosbury,[48] was presumably Coke's curate. In his will, dated 1690, Coke stated his resolution 'to live and die in the religion now professed in the Church of England'. He asked for burial, 'in the most private manner that may be', under the communion table in the chancel of Bosbury church, where he was buried early in 1691.[49]

Coke's successor, Joshua Elmhurst, had been master of the grammar school since 1684.[50] Like most of the 18th-century vicars, he was a graduate. The only one with a higher degree was William Allen, vicar 1777–94, who held a doctorate in divinity. He was a pluralist, being perpetual curate of Sutton St. Michael from 1775 to 1809, and he also held a prebend at Hereford cathedral. Curates, perhaps assistant curates, were appointed to Bosbury between 1775 and 1781.[51] In 1716 and 1719 the vicar, Humphrey Wynne, and the churchwardens reported that the church was well equipped for worship; services were held at 10 a.m. and 3 p.m. on Sundays, and communion was administered four times a year. They knew of no dissenters or recusants in 1716, but in 1719 reported one family of dissenters who attended services conducted by 'Mr Philips' in Bromyard.[52]

The 19th Century and Later

Curates were appointed in 1824, 1828, and 1830, during the long incumbency of John Lodge (vicar 1801–30); the first at least was required to live in the parish and was presumably curate in charge. It was during Lodge's time as vicar that Nonconformist meetings were first recorded in the parish. Another curate was appointed in 1856 or 1857, possibly to serve the church during a vacancy between the incumbencies of J.H. Underwood (1830–56) and B.L.S. Stanhope (1856–66).[53]

In 1851 Underwood reported a congregation of 379 in a church which could seat 470; he attributed the relatively poor attendance to the absence of people visiting parents and grandparents outside the parish for Mothering Sunday.[54] Underwood himself was an active parish priest, instigating and funding the first major restoration of the church building in 1851. In 1850 a newspaper noted the 'usual generosity' with which he had supported a parish dinner at the Crown Inn.[55] He claimed that in the 14 years he had been Rural Dean of Frome deanery, in which Bosbury lay, he had restored all

47   TNA, PROB 11/297, will of Joyce Bacon, 1660; PROB 11/309, will of Anthony Turnor, 1662; HAS, 58/1/76, will of Henry Broye, 1661. On the portioners of Bromyard, see Phyllis Williams, *Bromyard Minster, Manor and Town* (privately printed 1987), 20, 25.

48   HAS, AL19/20, f. 65.

49   HAS, 110/3/3, will of William Coke, 1690; Par. Rec., burials Feb. 1690/1.

50   HAS, AL19/20, f. 28.

51   http://www.theclergydatabase.org.uk (accessed 26 Oct. 2015).

52   HAS, HD5/14/100; HD5/15/25.

53   http://www.theclergydatabase.org.uk, s.v. Bosbury (accessed 26 Oct. 15); HAS, HD10/23 (diocesan year boxes). For the incumbents see A.T. Bannister, *Diocese of Hereford, Institutions 1539–1900*, 129, 171; Par. Rec., vestry bk. vol. 3, 30 Jun. 1830. On Nonconformity see below, this section.

54   TNA, HO 129/346.

55   HAS, HD10/23 (diocesan year box 1841); Par. Rec., vestry min. bk. vol. 2, 1848; *Hereford Times* 3 May 1851; *The Times* 2 Sept. 1856 (obituary); *Hereford Jnl*, 9 Jan. 1850: http://www.bosburyhistoryresource. org.uk (accessed 26 Oct. 2015).

the churches there. He became a prebendary of Hereford Cathedral.[56] Underwood's successor, the Hon. B.L.S. Stanhope, was a member of the Stanhope family of Holme Lacy. A former fellow of All Souls' College, Oxford, he later became archdeacon of Hereford.[57]

J.E. Cheese, almost certainly a member of a Kington family, became vicar in 1866.[58] He was conspicuous for his evangelical enthusiasm, and for the next 13 years his activities can be traced in the local newspapers. One of his first acts was to create a new choir at Bosbury, augmented by women. It was one of the largest choirs present at the Festival of Parish Choirs held in Hereford in August 1867. Services at Holy Trinity took on a new dimension, the lessons being intoned and responses sung to a setting by the 16th-century composer Thomas Tallis. A harvest festival was introduced in 1867 as a means of bringing the rural community together. The importance of music was demonstrated in 1875 when the eminent High Anglican musician and composer, Sir Frederick Arthur Gore Ouseley, precentor of Hereford Cathedral, directed the harvest festival service, bringing with him J.C. Ward, organist of Quebec Chapel in London.[59] Clearly, Cheese was determined to recover some of the congregation that were absent in 1851 and may have been attracted to the new Wesleyan Methodist chapel at Stanley Hill. His sympathy for the labouring classes is demonstrated by his support for and attendance at the Bosbury agricultural show, founded in 1847.[60]

Samuel Bentley, vicar 1879–97, had already published two volumes of sermons before he came to Bosbury; while there he published two histories of the parish: *Short Account of the Church and Episcopal Manor of Bosbury*, in 1881, and a longer *History and Description of the Parish of Bosbury* in 1891.[61] His successor, Robert Bayly, was the brother of the novelist 'Edna Lyall' (Ada Ellen Bayly, d. 1903), who was a frequent visitor to the vicarage and whose ashes were buried in the churchyard.[62]

Gifts of altar hangings in 1932 and of standard candlesticks in 1937 suggest moderate high churchmanship in the earlier 20th century.[63] The Second World War caused difficulties: in 1942 the PCC noted that income was declining, partly because of the loss of some generous benefactors, and in the same year the elderly vicar, H.K.L. Mathews, resigned, to make way for a younger and stronger man.[64] The high church practices of his successors in the 1960s and 1970s may not have been popular with parishioners, for when the living became vacant in 1978 they asked for a priest who was neither high nor low church, also one of 'ecumenical outlook' and 'pastoral inclination'.[65]

56   Obituary in *The Times* 2 Sept. 1856; *Hereford Times*, 3 May 1851.

57   *The Times*, 24 March 1919, Times digital archive, accessed 26 Oct. 2015.

58   *The Times* 6 Oct. 1866; *Littlebury's Dir. Herefs.* (1867), 53; J.B. Sinclair and R.D. Fenn, *The Border Janus: a new Kington history* (1995), 13–4, 37–8.

59   *Hereford Times*, 19 Oct. 1867, 22 Jun. 1867, 26 Oct. 1867; HAS, AS94/161.

60   *Hereford Times*, 26 Jan. 1867, 20 Jul. 1867. For the show see above, Social History.

61   S. Bentley, *Six Sermons on Prayer* (Bridgnorth, 1868); idem, *Parish Sermons* (London, 1875).

62   J.M. Escreet, *The life of Edna Lyall* (London: Longman, Green and Co., 1904), 257–9; *Glouc. Citizen*, 16 Feb. 1903: http://www.bosburyhistoryresource.org.uk (accessed 26 Oct. 2015); above, Introduction.

63   *Church Calendar and Clergy List for the Diocese of Hereford* (1932), 158; ibid. (1937), 160.

64   Par. Rec., PCC min. 1937–65, meetings of 16 Apr., 1 July 1942; *Church Calendar and Clergy List for Diocese of Hereford* (1941), p. 116 (s.v. Hugh K.L. Mathews).

65   Par. Rec., service registers, *passim*; Par. Rec., file on vacancy 1978–9.

Figure 18 *Samuel Bentley, vicar 1879–97, author of two histories of the parish.*

In 1920 it was agreed that the charity of Ann Jenkins (d. 1906) be applied to pay choir men in Bosbury Church, but by 1958 there were difficulties in using the money, presumably because of lack of choir men, and by 2008 the charity had ceased to operate.[66]

The Church of the Holy Trinity

The church, whose dedication to the Holy Trinity was first recorded in 1601,[67] comprises a chancel and a nave with north and south aisles, south-east chapel, and south porch; the detached tower stands in the churchyard *c.*60 ft. south of the south aisle. Only the west wall of the nave, with a round-arched window, remains of an aisleless 12th-century church, but the walls of that church were found in 1921–2 during excavations for a new heating system.[68] The surviving nave and the aisles with their fine arcades with trumpet-scallop capitals, pointed arches and lancet windows, all appear to date from *c.*1200 or earlier , and the exterior corbel table above the clerestory seems to confirm that date. All the doorways are round-arched, but the main south doorway combines this archaic feature with the more up-to-date capitals, confirming the Transitional character of the work. The core of the chancel is of the same date, with a chancel arch complementing the nave arcade, and mainly lancet windows in its north and south walls. The south porch

66   Par. Rec., vestry min. vol. 4, 6 Apr. 1920; 8 Apr. 1958; http://www.charitycommissioners.gov.uk (accessed 18 Dec. 2015).
67   HAS, 7/2/27, will of John Bowley, 1601.
68   RCHME, *Herefordshire*, ii. 10, 17, 61, 141; *TWNFC* (1923), p. cvii.

Figure 19 *Holy Trinity church and its detached tower, 2015; the Morton chapel can be seen protruding from the south side of the church.*

was added in the 15th century, and late in the same century the triple lancet east window was replaced by a Perpendicular one.

The massive detached tower, of three stages with its lancet windows and north doorway with two-centred head, was built *c*.1230–40. It is one of at least 14 such towers originally built in Herefordshire, of which seven are still detached, the highest number for any county in England. At 60 ft. from the south wall of the (later) Morton chapel, the Bosbury tower is the furthest of the towers from the main church fabric, and, like some of the others, is on a slightly different alignment from the church. There is no obvious reason for its construction in that position, unless it had some sort of defensive functions or was intended to serve as a refuge as well as a bell tower.[69]

The south-east or Morton chapel was added to the end of the south aisle in the early 16th century; the exterior has battlements, buttresses and wide Perpendicular windows. Inside, the chapel is illuminated by windows with uniform mouldings. Against the wall of the south arcade there is a similar panelled arch, all of which modulate into a small fan-vault, which frames two quatrefoils embracing a 'tun' – the Morton rebus – embellished

69   RCHME, *Herefordshire*. ii, 17; Brooks and Pevsner, *Herefordshire*, 29, 115–16; G. Marshall, 'The detached church towers of Herefordshire', *TWNFC* (1943), 133–4.

Figure 20 *Interior of
the Morton chapel
2016, showing the
Perpendicular windows.*

with the capital 'M'. Elsewhere the 'tun' is carved as a pendent with the initials 'T.M.' for
the founder, Thomas Morton.

In the 1670s the bishop's court rolls regularly recorded that the chancel was 'out of
repair' or in 'great decay'.[70] In 1716, however, the roofs, walls, windows and floor were all
reported to be in good condition.[71] A timber spire on the tower was struck by lightning in
1638; it was repaired in 1758, and 1769, and removed in 1815.[72]

The process of restoration began in 1804 when Richard Jones, a Ledbury surveyor,
superintended the re-roofing and re-plastering of the nave. In 1844 the *Worcester Journal*
noticed the re-opening of the church after 'extensive alterations and improvements to
restore the interior . . . to its pristine proportions'.[73] Details of the work remain obscure:
but a new floor was clearly involved since the Early English font was removed and

70   e.g. HAS, AA63/2, pp. 185; AA63/3, pp. 24, 79.
71   HAS, HD5/14/100.
72   Par. Rec., vestry min. vol. 1, pp. 65, 132; vol. 2, p. 28; Bentley, *Short Account of Bosbury* (1881), 15;
     Hereford Jnl, 3 May 1815, http://www.bosburyhistoryresource.org.uk (accessed 2 Jan. 2016).
73   Par. Rec, vestry min., vol. 2, pp. 14–15; *Berrow's Worcester Jnl*, 30 May 1844, 6 June 1844.

Figure 21 *The church and tower, 1717. The round-headed windows are inaccurate, but demonstrate the total lack of sympathy for gothic and the aspiration for classical simplicity at that date.*

restored, under the west gallery, with new pillars on a raised pedestal. During the work the 11th-century or earlier font was discovered, buried upside down, immediately below the existing font.[74] An 'ancient lectern . . . similar to ones seen in cathedrals and colleges', which occupied the centre of the nave was also restored, but has since been lost; it sounds like a Jacobean pulpit.[75]

Further work was carried out, mainly in the chancel, in 1851. The ceiling was removed and 'open woodwork', 'ribbed, stained and varnished', was inserted. Stained glass by George Rogers of Worcester was put into the north and south lancet windows.[76] A 'handsome' pulpit and reading desk incorporating carved oak panels from a 'religious house in Flanders' were made, and the chancel screen, 'much injured' by the collapsing roof of the chancel, was restored by Mr Freame, a Worcester cabinet maker. The church was re-opened on 24 April 1851.[77] In the winter of 1859–60 the nave was apparently reroofed, although the modest cost of £300 suggests that the architect, Thomas Nicholson, simply took away the ceiling and repaired the existing 13th-century roof.[78]

74   Bryant and Hare, *Corpus of Anglo-Saxon Stone Sculpture: W. Midlands* X, 283–4; S. Bentley, 'Church and manor of Bosbury', *TWNFC* (1894), 181.

75   *Berrow's Worcester Jnl*, 6 Jun. 1844.

76   They were replaced 1880–2 by new windows by Waile and Strange: Brooks and Pevsner, *Herefordshire*, 116.

77   *Hereford Jnl*, 7 May 1851; *Hereford Times*, 3 May 1851.

78   Par. Rec., vestry min. bk. vol. 4, meeting 8 July 1859; RCHM, *Herefs.*, ii. 19.

A major restoration, largely financed by Edward Higgins of Bosbury House, was carried out in 1871, during the incumbency of J.E. Cheese. The architect was Ewan Christian, favourite architect of the Church Commissioners and of the Cambridge Camden Society's journal, the *Ecclesiologist*.[79] He rebuilt part of the east wall of the chancel, including the Perpendicular window. The stained glass by Wailes and Strang, which arrived in 1880, was given by Higgins in memory of his two grandsons.[80] Externally, the roof was raised to its 'correct' pitch; inside, the woodwork ceiling of 1851 was retained. An organ chamber was built on the north side of the chancel, possibly destroying a lancet window; this replaced the west gallery, which was removed. The chancel and nave floors were tiled with encaustic tiles from Godwin's of Lugwardine, and their walls were stripped and re-stuccoed. New oak seating was inserted in the choir, and some additional seats in the nave, which otherwise retained its earlier pews. The plain panelling behind the altar probably dates from this restoration. The south-east chapel and the porch were repaired.[81] In 1878 Cheese gave the clock on the south face of the tower.[82]

A fire in 1876 damaged the roof, and a more serious one in 1917 damaged both the roof and the west end of the nave.[83] Repairs following the 1917 fire commenced in 1921, supervised by the architect W.D. Caröe, architect to the Church Commissioners. He rebuilt the south aisle wall to the west of the porch, adding a small three-light Perpendicular window to light the baptistery. At the same time he reinforced the walls and foundations of the chancel, and strengthened the west front with steel bars. A vestry was created by inserting screens at the west end of the north aisle, an inner porch built, and the west end of the church panelled in oak.[84]

Regular repairs were carried out in the 20th century, including work on the south-east (Morton) chapel in 1922, and in 1986 when it was completely re-glazed; the church roof was overhauled in 1961, and the chancel in 1973–4. In 2014 the church was placed on the English Heritage (now Historic England) 'at risk' register for urgent repairs required to the roof of the north aisle and the tower, and work to deal with ground-level damp.[85]

There are two early Renaissance monuments in the chancel: that to John Harford (d. 1559) is signed by John Guldo (Gildon) of Hereford; the second to Richard Harford (d. 1578) is unsigned and coarser in character. Both make confident use of classical detail and thus reflect the dawning of the Renaissance in the West Midlands.[86] Also in the chancel is a marble tablet to John Brydges of Old Colwall (d. 1742). On the south wall of

79   *The Builder*, Jul. 1871; S. Muthesius, *The High Victorian Movement in Architecture, 1850–1870* (1972), 53, 201.
80   Bentley, 'Church and manor', 180.
81   *The Builder*, July 1871; *Littlebury's Dir. Herefs.* (1876); Bentley, *Short Account of Bosbury*, preface, 13; Par. Rec., Caröe's 1917 report.
82   *Kelly's Dir. Herefs.* (1885).
83   *Berrow's Worcester Jnl*, 15 Jan. 1876.
84   Par. Rec., papers including Caröe's report, Dec. 1917 and report and balance sheet Nov. 1922; *Kelly's Dir. Herefs.* (1934); *TWNFC* (1923), pp. cvi–cviii.
85   Par. Rec., Bellamy's contracts; Worcs. R.O, 705:876; ibid. BA8077/23/ii; *Historic England Heritage at Risk, W. Midlands Reg.* (London, 2015); notice in church (Sept. 2015). Repairs began in spring 2016.
86   K.A. Esdaile, *English Monumental Sculpture since the Renaissance* (1927), 13–14; L. Butler, 'John Gildon of Hereford: a late sixteenth-century sculptor', *Archaeol. Jnl*, 129 (1972), 148–53.

Figure 22 *Tomb of John Harford (d. 1559), 2015. The monument was designed by John Guldo (Gildon) of Hereford.*

the nave is a fragmentary medieval inscription, found in 1746, noticing Bishop Richard Swinfield's father, Stephen.[87]

The vicar George Wall left money in 1641 towards casting a new bell, perhaps the surviving fifth which had been cast the previous year by John Finch of Hereford. The other bells are: treble (1903), second (1632, recast 1939), third (1681), fourth (probably 16th-century, recast 1937), and tenor (1660).[88]

An organ by T.C. Bates of London, installed in 1844, was replaced in 1871 by a large instrument by Speechly and Ingram of the Camden Works, London, given by Mrs. Hope, sister-in-law of Edward Higgins.[89]

The rectangular churchyard was slightly reduced in size in 1796 when the vicar, T.F. Otley, annexed four yards to the vicarage garden. He also had the lych gate moved to its present position opposite the church door. It had presumably earlier stood on the

87 I. Roscoe (ed.), *A Bibliographical Dictionary of Sculptors in Britain, 1660–1851* (2009), 1374–5; HAS, CF50/116, between 378 and 379.

88 HAS, 54/2/21, will of George Wall, 1641; F. Sharpe, *Church Bells of Herefordshire*, I (1966), 74–5.

89 *Berrow's Worcester Jnl*, 30 May 1844, 6 Jun. 1844; *The Builder*, July 1871; *Littlebury's Dir. Herefs.* (1876); Par. Rec., Caröe's 1917 report.

vicarage boundary, as in 1769 the vicar had used it as a pigeon loft.[90] A 15th-century churchyard cross base, rising with steps to a square plinth, supports a modern shaft and a cross-head which probably dates from the mid 17th century; it was seriously damaged and repaired in 1949.[91] A new extension to the graveyard, on land opposite Old Court (formerly the boys' school playground) was opened in 1998.[92]

Nonconformity

United Brethren, later Mormons

There is evidence of dissenting activity in the village from 1815, when licences were granted to William Pritchard and George Davies to use their houses for religious worship. Between 1832 and 1836 a further four licences were granted, three of which were supported by Thomas Kington of Castle Frome. Kington was a member of the United Brethren and was among those reputed to have joined the Latter Day Saints (Mormons) during their mission to the area in 1840.[93] A Mormon missionary based at Castle Frome preached at Stanley Hill in 1840, and a house there was subsequently used for Mormon services. A number of converts from Bosbury later emigrated to the United States.[94]

Methodists

A building called the Wesleyan chapel in Bosbury parish was licensed in 1839. In 1851, however, the Wesleyan Methodists had no separate building; 22 people attended afternoon worship and 28 the evening service. A freehold brick-built chapel was erected at the top of Stanley Hill in 1863 and registered in 1865.[95] The chapel was part of the Ledbury Circuit with meetings led by ministers from the circuit. (Another chapel at Upleadon, possibly that at Swinmore discussed below, was also listed as part of the circuit.) The craftsman Philip Clissett, who lived close by, was among trustees appointed in 1899.[96] The chapel is listed in the 1941 Kelly's Directory but was sold in 1954.[97] By 2015 it was unoccupied and derelict.

The chapel building was designed by William Willmer Pocock, architect of Spurgeon's Metropolitan Tabernacle at the Elephant and Castle, London. The rectangular building, of polychrome brick in Gothic style, was described at its opening as 'the handsomest chapel in the Ledbury circuit'. It seated c.150. Alterations of an unknown character were made, or proposed, in 1927.[98]

---

90   Par. Rec., vestry mins. vol. 1, p. 169.
91   Par. Rec., PCC mins. 14 Jul. 1949; see above, Introduction.
92   Ex inf. Barry Sharples.
93   HAS, CA19/2; HAS, HD8/9, HD8/11a; HD8/14; *VCH Glos.* XII, 172.
94   http://www.bosburyhistoryresource.org.uk (accessed 30 Oct. 2015), for material including W. Woodruff, *Leaves from my Journal* (1882), 77–82; *The Latter-Day Saints Millenial Star*, vol. 1, no. 1, 86–9.
95   HAS, HD 8/13; HAS, AL 29/11; HAS, AA18/37; TNA, HO 129/343.
96   HAS, AL 29/11, AL 29/12.
97   *Kelly's Dir. Herefs.* (1941); HAS, AA18/37.
98   HER, 26801; HAS, K21.

The religious census return in 1851 noted that Primitive Methodists had been meeting in rooms at Swinmore Common from 1844; 18 people were recorded at morning worship and 41 at the evening service. A chapel measuring c.15 ft. by 22 ft designed to hold between 80–100 worshippers was under construction. The brick-built building stood beside the road which ran along the edge of the common.[99] In 1881 William Bury of the nearby Verne Farm was a farmer and Methodist preacher. Correspondence with the Methodist minister in Ledbury suggests the chapel may have become part of the Wesleyan circuit sometime after 1915. Another letter, in 1921, refers to notice of the termination of the tenancy of the chapel. Nevertheless the chapel was listed in Directories until 1941.[100] By 2008 the unoccupied building was abandoned.[101]

Plymouth Brethren

The Plymouth Brethren met in the village between 1895 and 1917.[102] They occupied a rectangular, probably single-roomed, brick building in the centre of the village. For some years in the 1920s the chapel was used for Baptist services, led by the shopkeeper Uriah Cosford.[103] Between 1921 and 1941 it was listed in Directories as a free church hall.[104] In the later 20th century it was converted into a dwelling.

---

99 TNA, HO 129/343; OS Map, 1887, http://www.bosburyhistoryresource.org.uk (accessed 13 Oct. 2015).
100 TNA, RG 11/2581; HAS, AA18/37; *Kelly's Dir. Herefs.* (1941).
101 B. Pardoe, 'Rapid buildings survey abandoned chapels of the Ledbury district: Swinmoor Common', unpubl. typescript 2008.
102 *Jakeman & Carver Dir. Herefs.* (1895); *Kelly's Dir. Herefs* (1917).
103 *Grantham Jnl*, 2 May 1931, obituary of Uriah Cosford, http://www.bosburyhistoryresource.org.uk (accessed 15 Dec. 2015).
104 *Kelly's Dir. Herefs.* (1941).

NOTE ON SOURCES

This note discusses the main manuscript and printed sources used in writing the history of Bosbury. It is not comprehensive, and should be used in conjunction with the List of Abbreviations.

Manuscript Sources

Public Repositories

The **Herefordshire Archive Service** holds the records of county government (including inclosure awards and 18th- and 19th-century land tax assessments), the Hereford diocesan and archidiaconal records (including bishops' registers, documents relating to the administration of the bishop's estates, and church terriers), and nonconformist records. It also has a large collection of private records including charters and accounts.

The principal documents used in this history are:

A63/III/23/1:	Rental of Hospitallers' manors 1504–5
A81/II/83–102:	Bosbury estate records of the Brydges family of Tibberton
AA63:	Court books for the bishop's manors, 1661 onwards
AA59 A1:	Rental of the bishop's manors, *c*.1288
AA59 A2:	Survey of the bishop's estates by Swithun Butterfield, 1577
AM33:	Bailiffs' accounts and court records for the bishop's manors, 1497–1592
AS94:	Records of the Homes family of Bosbury
HD1/4–6:	Records of the bishop's Bosbury estate
HD4/1	Court books for the diocese of Hereford
HD5, HD8, HD10:	Diocesan records, mainly relating to parish clergy and parish administration
M5:	Sale particulars
Q:	Records of Quarter Sessions, responsible for county administration from the 16th to the 19th centuries, including Q/REL (Land tax assessments from 1787)

Local wills proved in the diocesan court in the 16th and 17th centuries; these are numbered in the form 9/3/46, with no preliminary letters.

The **Herefordshire Environment Record** (formerly the Sites and Monuments Record) holds notes of archaeological sites and features and of listed buildings. It is accessible at Herefordshire Through Time: http://htt.herefordshire.gov.uk/27.aspx.

The **Hereford Cathedral Library** holds the cathedral archives including early charters and transcripts of the Chapter Act Books.

The National Archives at Kew, London, hold the records of national government from the late 12th century onwards. Calendars of some medieval administrative records which have been used in this history, notably the Close and Patent Rolls, have been published. The classes of documents used in this history include:

C:	Records of the court of Chancery, including C1, Legal proceedings in the court of Chancery, 1386–1558
C 6:	Legal proceedings in the court of Chancery 1625–1714
E 199:	Exchequer King's Remembrancer and Lord Treasurer's Remembrancer, Sheriffs' accounts, Petitions etc.
E 358:	Exchequer, Pipe Office, Miscellaneous Enrolled Accounts
HO 107:	Home Office, Census Enumerators' returns, 1841, 1851
HO 129:	Home Office, Ecclesiastical census 1851
LR 3:	Office of the auditors of land revenue: court rolls of crown manors
MAF 48:	Agriculture, Fisheries and Food departments and related bodies, land correspondence and papers
MAF 174:	Ministry of Agriculture and Fisheries and Ministry of Agriculture, Fisheries and Food: Worcester Divisional Office: Registered files
PROB 11:	Records of the Prerogative Court of Canterbury, registers of wills proved 1384–1858
RG 9–14:	General Register Office, Census Enumerators' returns 1861–1911
SC 6:	Special Collections, Ministers' and Receivers' Accounts for estates in the possession of the Crown

Transcripts of all the census enumerators' returns are available at http://www. bosburyhistoryresource.org.uk/menu-villagers.

All the **Parish Records** are in the parish church. Transcripts of the baptism, marriage and burial registers are available at http://www.bosburyhistoryresource.org.uk/menu-parish-registers.html.

Printed Sources

Primary Sources

The most important printed primary sources, including calendars of major classes in The National Archives are included in the List of Abbreviations. The *Registers* of Bishops Cantilupe, Orleton, Thomas and Lewis Charlton, Trillek, Courtenay, Gilbert, Trefnant,

Mascall, Lacy, Polton, Spofford, Beauchamp, Boulers, Stanbury, Milling, Mayew and Booth, which were printed by the Cantilupe Society between 1906 and 1921, contain information about Bosbury manor as well as about the church.

Copies of Herefordshire Trade Directories, including Kelly's, are available online at http://specialcollections.le.ac.uk/cdm/landingpage/collection/p16445coll4; others are to be found in the Herefordshire Archive Services' Library and in the Herefordshire Libraries collections.

The other published primary sources used in this history are:
English Episcopal Acta xxxv. *Hereford 1234–75*, ed. J. Barrow (London, 2009)
Calendar of Probate and Administration Acts 1407–1550 in the Consistory Court of the Bishops of Hereford, ed. M.A. Faraday (Logaston, 2008)
Herefordshire Militia Assessments of 1663, ed. M.A. Faraday (Camd. 4th ser. x)
Herefordshire taxes in the reign of Henry VIII, ed. M.A. Faraday (Hereford, 2005)
The Herefordshire Chantry Valuations of 1547, ed. M.A. Faraday (privately printed, 2012)
Roll of the Household Expenses of Richard de Swinfield bishop of Hereford during part of the years 1289 and 1290, ed. J. Webb (Camden Soc., 1855)

The tithe maps for all Herefordshire parishes including Bosbury, have been privately published by Geoff Gwatkin. Copies of the maps, which incorporate place-names and other material from the tithe awards, are available in Herefordshire libraries and at Herefordshire Archives and Record Centre (HARC), Fir Tree Lane, Rotherwas, Hereford.

Books

The most important secondary sources for the history of Bosbury are the two books by the vicar Samuel Bentley, *A Short Account of the Church, Episcopal Manor and other objects of interest in Bosbury Herefordshire* (London, 1881), and *History and Description of the parish of Bosbury in the diocese of Hereford* (London, 1891).

Two 19th-century works on Herefordshire history have been used: M.G. Watkins, *Collections for the History and Antiquities of Herefordshire, Radlow Hundred* (1902, bound as Duncomb's *Herefordshire* vol. 5) and C.J. Robinson, *Mansions and Manors of Herefordshire* (1873, reprinted Logaston, 2001).

The main sources for architectural history are A. Brooks and N. Pevsner, *Herefordshire* (The Buildings of England, 2012) and Royal Commission on Historical Monuments (England), *An Inventory of the Historical Monuments in Herefordshire*, vol. 2 East (HMSO, 1932).

Website

The website http://www.bosburyhistoryresource.org.uk, compiled by Barry Sharples, contains transcripts of numerous sources for the history of Bosbury, including extracts from newspapers, early maps, and photographs, as well as the documents noted above.

ABBREVIATIONS

The following abbreviations and short titles have been used.

Bentley, *Short Account of Bosbury* (1881)	Samuel Bentley, *A Short Account of the Church, Episcopal Manor and other objects of interest in Bosbury Herefordshire* (London, 1881)
Bentley, *Hist. Bosbury* (1891)	Samuel Bentley, *History and Description of the parish of Bosbury in the diocese of Hereford* (London, 1891)
Bk.	book
Bk. of Fees	*The Book of Fees* (HMSO, 1920–31)
BL	British Library
Cal.	Calendar
Cal. Chart. R.	*Calendar of the Charter Rolls preserved in the Public Record Office* (HMSO, 1903–27)
Cal. Close	*Calendar of the Close Rolls preserved in the Public Record Office* (HMSO, 1892–1963)
Cal. Fine R.	*Calendar of the Fine Rolls preserved in the Public Record Office* (HMSO, 1911–62)
Cal. Inq. Misc.	*Calendar of Inquisitions Miscellaneous (Chancery) preserved in the Public Record Office* (HMSO, 1916–68)
Cal. Inq. p.m.	*Calendar of Inquisitions post mortem preserved in the Public Record Office* (HMSO, 1904–2010)
Cal. Papal Reg.	*Calendar of the Papal Registers: Papal Letters* (HMSO and Irish MSS Com., 1891–2005)
Cal. Pat.	*Calendar of the Patent Rolls preserved in the Public Record Office* (HMSO, 1890–1986)
Cal. S.P. Dom.	*Calendar of State Papers, Domestic Series* (HMSO, 1856–1972)
Cat.	catalogue
Cat. Anct. D.	*Descriptive Catalogue of Ancient Deeds in the Public Record Office* (HMSO, 1890–1915)
Cur. Reg. R.	*Curia Regis Rolls preserved in the Public Record Office* (HMSO, 1922–79)

Dir.	*Directory*
Domesday	A. Williams and G.H. Martin (eds.), *Domesday Book: A Complete Translation* (London, 2002)
EHR	*English Historical Review*
EPNS	English Place-Name Society
Feud. Aids	*Inquisitions and assessments relating to Feudal Aids preserved in the Public Record Office* (HMSO, 1899–1920)
HAS	Herefordshire Archive Service (formerly Herefordshire Record Office)
HCA	Hereford Cathedral Archives, Cathedral Library, Hereford
HER	Historic Environment Record (formerly SMR or Sites and Monuments Record) at Herefordshire Through Time: http://htt.herefordshire.gov.uk
Hist.	History/Historical
Hist. MSS Com.	Royal Commission on Historical Manuscripts
HMSO	His (Her) Majesty's Stationery Office
Inf.	information
Jnl.	Journal
L & P Hen. VIII	*Letters and Papers, Foreign and Domestic, of the Reign of Henry VIII* (HMSO, 1864–1932)
Libr.	Library
Min.	minute/minutes
Mun.	muniments
NHL	National Heritage List for England (http://www.historicengland.org.uk/listing/the-list/)
NMR	National Monuments Record (Swindon)
OS	Ordnance Survey
ODNB	*Oxford Dictionary of National Biography* (Oxford, 2004), http://www.oxforddnb.com
Par. Rec.	Parish records held in Bosbury parish church
P.O.	Post Office
PRS	Pipe Roll Society
RCHME	Royal Commission on Historical Monuments (England)
RO	Record Office
Rec. Com.	Record Commission
Reg. Bothe	*The Register of Charles Bothe, Bishop of Hereford 1516–1535*, ed. A.T. Bannister (Hereford, 1921)

Reg. Cantilupe	*The Register of Thomas de Cantilupe, Bishop of Hereford 1275–1282*, ed. W.W. Capes (Hereford, 1906)
Reg. Gilbert	*The Register of John Gilbert, Bishop of Hereford 1375–1389*, ed. J.H. Parry (Hereford, 1913)
Reg. Lacy	*The Register of Edmund Lacy, Bishop of Hereford 1417–1420*, ed. A.T. Bannister (Hereford, 1917)
Reg. Mayew	*The Register of Richard Mayew, Bishop of Hereford 1504–1516*, ed. A.T. Bannister (Hereford, 1919)
Reg. Myllyng	*The Register of Thomas Myllyng, Bishop of Hereford 1474–1492*, ed. A.T. Bannister (Hereford, 1919)
Reg. Stanbury	*The Register of John Stanbury, Bishop of Hereford 1453–1474*, ed. J.H. Parry (Hereford, 1918)
Reg. Spofford	*The Register of Thomas Spofford, Bishop of Hereford 1422–1448*, ed. A.T. Bannister (1Hereford, 919)
Reg. Ric. Swinfield	*The Register of Richard de Swinfield, Bishop of Hereford 1283–1317*, ed. W.W. Capes (Hereford, 1909)
Reg. Thomas Charlton	*The Register of Thomas de Charlton, Bishop of Hereford 1327–1344*, ed. W.W. Capes (Hereford, 1909)
Reg. Trefnant	*The Register of John Trefnant, Bishop of Hereford 1389–1404*, ed. W.W. Capes (Hereford, 1914)
Reg. Trilleck	*The Register of John de Trilleck, Bishop of Hereford 1344–1361*, ed. J.H. Parry (Hereford, 1910)
Robinson, *Mansions and Manors*	C.J. Robinson, *The Mansions of Herefordshire and their Manors* (1872)
Soc.	Society
TNA	The National Archives
TS	Typescript
TWNFC	*Transactions of the Woolhope Naturalists' Field Club*

GLOSSARY

The following technical terms may require explanation. Fuller information on local history topics is available in D. Hey, *The Oxford Companion to Local and Family History* (2nd edn, 2010), or online from the VCH website: http://www.victoriacountyhistory. ac.uk. The most convenient glossary of architectural terms is *Pevsner's Architectural Glossary* (2010), now also available for iPhone and iPad.

bay: in architecture, a unit of a building inside or out regularly divided from the next by features such as columns or windows. Can apply to a window projecting from a bay.

Black Death: outbreak of bubonic plague which killed about a third of the population of England in 1348–9.

common (open) fields: communal agrarian organization under which an individual's farmland was held in strips scattered amongst two or more large fields, intermingled with strips of other tenants. Management of the fields and usually common meadows and pasture was regulated through the manor court or other communal assembly.

copyhold: form of land tenure granted in a manor court, so called because the tenant received a 'copy' of the grant as noted in the court records. Often given for several lives (e.g. tenant, wife, and eldest child).

customary tenure: unfree or copyhold tenure regulated by local manorial custom.

demesne: in the Middle Ages, land farmed directly by a lord of the manor, rather than granted to tenants. Though usually leased out from the later Middle Ages, demesne lands often remained distinct from the rest of a parish's land.

forlet land: originally those parts of the bishop of Hereford's demesne land which were let to tenants for the life of the bishop for the time being. By the late 16th century the term was used more generally for a leasehold tenure.

glebe: land assigned to the rector (q.v.) or vicar (q.v.) of a church for his support and the endowment of the church.

hearth tax: royal tax imposed in 1662 and 1665, assessed on the number of hearths or fireplaces in each taxpayer's house.

hide: unit of land measurement: in the early Anglo-Saxon period the amount required for a family to subsist on; in Domesday Book (1086), a taxation unit; and by the 13th century the sum of 4 yardlands (q.v.).

Hospitallers: members of the military-religious order of the Knights of the Hospital of St John of Jerusalem who held extensive lands in England and elsewhere in Europe.

inclosure: the process whereby open fields was divided into fields, to be redistributed among the various tenants and landholders. From the 18th century usually by an Act of Parliament obtained by the dominant landowners; earlier, more commonly done by private agreement, or by a powerful lord acting on his own initiative.

manor: a piece of landed property with tenants regulated by a private (manor) court. Originally held by feudal tenure, manors descended through a succession of heirs but could be given away or sold.

messuage: portion of land or a holding, generally with a house and outbuildings on it.

parish: the area attached to a parish church and owing tithes to it. From the Elizabethan period it had civil responsibilities, hence a 'civil' as opposed to an 'ecclesiastical' parish. At first the two were usually identical, but from the 19th century, when many parishes were reorganized, their boundaries sometimes diverged.

patron (of a church): the person having the right to nominate a candidate to the bishop for appointment as rector or vicar of a church. Often the lord of the manor, but the right could be bought and sold.

prebend: land or other property (including tithes) owned by a cathedral, and allocated in perpetuity to one of the cathedral's canons (or 'prebendaries').

rectory: (a) a church living served by a rector, who generally received the church's whole income; (b) the church's property or endowment (the rectory estate), comprising tithes, offerings, and usually some land or glebe.

recusant: a Roman Catholic who did not attend the services of the Church of England, as was required by law.

stint: the number of animals a tenant was allowed to graze on the common pastures, dictated by local custom, and enforced usually through the manor court.

Templars: members of the military-religious order founded as the Order of the Poor Knights of Christ and of the Temple of Solomon to protect pilgrims to the Holy Land. The order, which held extensive lands in England and elsewhere in Europe, was dissolved by papal order in 1312 after a five-year campaign against them led by Philip IV of France.

vestry: (a) in a church where clerical vestments are stored; (b) assembly of leading parishioners and ratepayers, responsible for poor relief and other secular matters as well as church affairs.

vicar: until the 19th century a clergyman appointed to act as priest of a parish, particularly as assistant to or substitute for the rector. He received a stipend or a proportion of the church's income.

vicarage: the endowment (often land or tithes) from which the vicar's stipend was paid.

yardland: the conventional holding of a medieval peasant, of 15–40 acres depending on local custom. Most generated surplus crops for sale at market, although those with fragments of yardlands probably needed to work part-time for better-off neighbours.

yeoman: from the 16th century, a term used for more prosperous farmers, many of them socially aspirational. The term husbandman usually denoted less well-off farmers.

INDEX

All places are in Herefordshire unless otherwise stated. All buildings, estates, institutions, etc. are in Bosbury unless otherwise stated. References to illustrations are in italics.

CPSIA information can be obtained
at www.ICGtesting.com
Printed in the USA
FSHW020534310321
79947FS

9 781909 646254